Models of America's Past

Models
of America's Past

And How to Make Them

C. J. MAGINLEY
Illustrated by Elisabeth D. McKee

HARCOURT, BRACE & WORLD, INC., NEW YORK

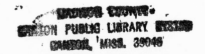

To my grandsons
Kevin B. Seymour and Geoffrey M. Seymour

Contents

Author's Note

This book is an attempt to help those who read it relive something of the past history of our country through the construction of models of things used by our forebears. Many of the objects described in these pages are miniatures of those articles made by our ancestors with their own hands and few tools. By constructing a little cradle, an old table, or a covered bridge, the modelmaker will be made more aware of life as it was in America in earlier times. He may appreciate more the contribution made by the rugged pioneers in laying the foundation for the America of today. He may even come to the conclusion that there is something to be said about life in the America of yesteryear and think that there really were "the good old days."

Making a model is also an excellent way to relax and to create with the hands what is conceived by the mind. All children, and adults as well, need to learn to use their hands skillfully, for working with the hands provides an outlet that no other activity supplies so well. Many enjoyable hours of leisure can be spent "whiling away time" building a model.

Introduction

Tools

The author assumes that only hand tools will be available to the model builder. The models described in this book can all be made with the tools listed below.

Coping saw
"Tiny Tim" hacksaw
Small hand drill
Twist drills, which should include numbers 45, 55, 57, 60, 66, $\frac{1}{16}''$, $\frac{1}{8}''$, $\frac{3}{16}''$
Small hammer
Pliers
Long-nose pliers
Wire cutters
Vise
Small files—flat, pointed, round, half-round
Try square
Ruler
Awl
Compass
Emery boards
Sandpaper—medium, fine
Sharp knife
Single-edge razor blades

Materials—Wood

Soft woods such as pine or basswood are best for making most of the parts for the models. Plywood, available at hobby stores in different thicknesses, is good for making parts where there is any danger of splitting, such as the rims for the wheels.

Balsa wood can be cut more easily than the pine or basswood but is very soft. However, when wood $\frac{1}{64}''$, $\frac{1}{32}''$, or $\frac{1}{16}''$ in thickness is needed, balsa wood is very good.

Small pieces of wood can often be obtained from the scrap pile at a cabinetmaker's shop, lumberyard, or woodworking plant. There are many "do-it-yourself" craftsmen with power tools who might also be a good source for small pieces of wood.

Materials—Miscellaneous

> White glue
> Rubber bands
> Common pins
> Number 24 pins
> Round toothpicks
> Flat toothpicks
> Paper clips
> Plastic-bag ties (paper-covered wire)
> Florist's wire
> Applicator sticks ($\frac{1}{16}''$ dowels)
> Transparent plastic—$\frac{1}{64}''$–$\frac{1}{32}''$ thick

Making Wheels

The Hub

Make the hub from a piece of $\frac{1}{4}''$ or $\frac{3}{8}''$ dowel. Cut a groove about $\frac{3}{32}''$ deep around the hub for the spokes to fit into. A saw cut can be made first and enlarged with a file. Make the groove before cutting the hub to the desired length. Drill a hole lengthwise through the center of the hub for the axle and another hole, the size of the spokes being used, through the hub in the opposite direction. This second hole should go through the hub where the groove was made. Taper one end of the hub with a file and sandpaper.

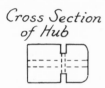

Cross Section of Hub

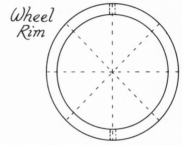

Wheel Rim

The Rim and Spokes

The best material to use for the rims of the wheels is $\frac{1}{8}''$, $\frac{3}{16}''$, or $\frac{1}{4}''$ plywood. Round toothpicks, applicator sticks, or $\frac{1}{16}''$ dowels can be used for the spokes.

When constructing a wheel, first draw a circle on the plywood with a compass. Draw an inner circle about $\frac{3}{16}''$ to $\frac{1}{4}''$ inside the first one. Before cutting out the disk, draw two or more diameters perpendicular to each other. These lines will be useful as guides when drilling the holes for the spokes. Saw out the disk and round off the edges with sandpaper. Divide the disk into eight or twelve equal parts, depending on the number of spokes to be used. Make a line on the circumference at the end of each radius. Then make a mark with an awl in the exact center of the circumference of the disk and drill holes for the spokes to a depth of $\frac{3}{8}''$ or so. Saw out the inner disk, leaving the rim of the wheel. Insert a piece of spoke material through the rim, the hole in the groove of the hub, and on through the rim on the other side. Center the hub on this spoke material. Insert other spokes through the remaining holes in the rim and into the groove, in which a little glue has been put. Cut off any protruding ends of spokes and finish with sandpaper.

Framed
Window

Installing Windows

Windows can be purchased at a hobby store in a variety of kinds and sizes. Some windows are printed on plastic, while others are molded from plastic or made of lead. The latter types, with the frame and sill, can be set into the openings and give the model a very finished appearance. The 3/8" by 5/8" window openings in all of the buildings described in this book are the size of the lead windows. The model builder will have to make any necessary changes in the size of the openings to conform to windows of a different size that he may buy.

When making the openings for windows, cut them a little smaller than the dimensions of the window being used and finish to the correct size with a flat file. The windows used by the author have twelve panes of "six over six." It is also a good idea to glue the windows in place before assembling the building.

If the printed windows are used, they should be glued

to the outside of the building over the opening and then a narrow frame of thin wood put around them.

Windows can be made by drawing lines to represent panes on fairly heavy plastic. Waxed paper can also be used and the panes outlined on it with a toothpick or pin. If waxed paper is used, it is best to fasten it to the inside of the building with tape and outline the panes afterward.

Making and Hanging Doors

1. Drill a hole, for a piece of paper clip or pin, through each door support $\frac{1}{16}''$ from one end. The supports should be as long as the door is wide.

2. Drill a slightly larger hole in each end of the door about $\frac{1}{4}''$ in depth and also $\frac{1}{16}''$ from one edge.

3. Drill a hole for the knob about $\frac{3}{16}''$ from the other edge and a little less than halfway up from the bottom of the door.

4. Glue the lower door support to the floor in front of the doorway.

5. Round off the corners of the edge of the door on the hinge side.

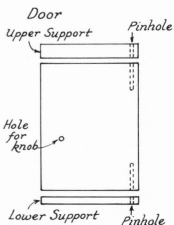

Door
Upper Support   Pinhole

Hole
for
knob

Lower Support   Pinhole

6. Insert a piece of pin or paper clip into the hole in the lower end of the door, letting it extend $\frac{1}{16}''$ or a little less.

7. Set the door in position with the wire in the hole in the support.

8. Glue the upper support directly above the lower one and a trifle above the end of the door so that it will not bind. Be sure that the holes in the supports and the door are in a straight line.

9. Insert a piece of wire down through the hole in the upper support into the hole in the door.

10. If the door binds, remove it and round off the edge a little more.

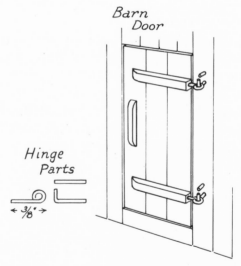

Barn
Door

Hinge
Parts

← ⅜" →

The Barn Doors

The doors for the barns can be made from one piece of wood or narrower pieces can be glued together to obtain the width needed. Make the doors a trifle narrower than the width given so that they will open and close easily.

The hinges, made from ⅛" by ⅛" wood, should be ⅛"

shorter than the width of the door. Glue the hinges to the door ¼″ from either end with one end of the hinge even with the edge of the door. The other end of the hinge should be rounded off with sandpaper. Drill a hole, slightly smaller than the wire being used for the eyes, in the center of the ends of the hinge. Make the eyes as shown in the drawing and insert them into the holes. The best way to make the eye is to put a small nail, with the point up, in the vise and bend the wire around it. Cut off one end of the U-shaped wire and bend the short end remaining around the nail to form the eye. Glue the handles to the doors about midway between the top and bottom and ⅛″ from the edges.

Set the doors temporarily in place and mark the location of the hangers. Drill holes for the hangers, which should be approximately ⅟₁₆″ from the edge of the doorframe. The hangers should fit snugly in the holes. In order to prevent the doors from coming off the hangers, a hole can be drilled, slightly above one of the eyes, and a piece of wire inserted into the hole.

Roofing the Buildings

When applying the roof boards, leave a little space between them and cover or box in the ends as follows:

Measure the distance from the peak of the roof to the end of a rafter. Glue a piece of wood ⅟₁₆″ by ¼″ (⅟₁₆″ x ½″ for stone barn) by the measured length to the underside of the roof boards where they extend beyond the ends of the barn or bridge. The piece will also be against the end. Measure and glue a second piece to the other side of the roof. These pieces will extend about ⅛″ beyond the ends of the roof boards. Glue strips ⅟₁₆″ by ⅛″ by the needed length, to the upper side of the first pieces where they extend beyond the ends of the roof boards. If the peak is a right angle, as the peaks of the barns and toll-house are, the pieces will not have to be cut at a 45-degree angle. The shorter piece will butt against the longer piece at the peak to form a right angle.

The pieces for the schoolhouse, meetinghouse, and bridges must be cut at the same angle or slant as the roof. The $\frac{1}{16}''$ by $\frac{1}{8}''$ wood must be the same thickness as the roof boards.

The ends of the roof boards on some old barns were not boxed in. This step may be omitted.

Applying Shingles

Cut the shingles $1''$ in length and in three or four different widths from $\frac{1}{4}''$ to $\frac{1}{2}''$. Use $\frac{1}{64}''$ material if available; the thinner the shingles are, the better. Starting at the lower edge of the roof, apply the first row, allowing the ends to extend an $\frac{1}{8}''$ or so at the lower edge of the roof. If $\frac{1}{32}''$ material is being used, when the glue has set, sandpaper the upper ends to make them thinner before putting the next row on. An emery board is good for this purpose. Leave a little space or crack between each shingle and place them so that $\frac{1}{2}''$ of each row is "exposed to the weather." Use shingles of varying widths so that the spaces or cracks between the shingles in one row are not in line with those in the preceding row.

It is a good plan to work first from one side of the roof and then the other to allow the glue to set. When near the peak, cut the shingles for the last rows to the length required so that they will meet from the two sides at the peak.

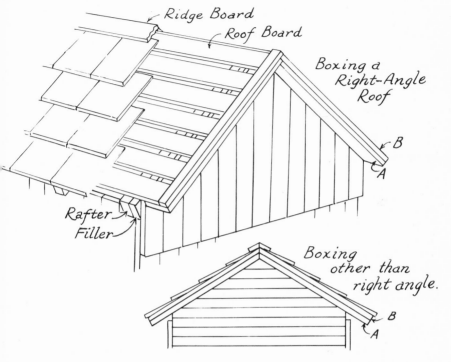

Glue a thin ridge board, as long as the building and ¼″ to ⅜″ wide, depending on the size of the structure, to each side of the peak. One of these boards should overlap the edge of the other.

Roofs can also be made in two pieces, one overlapping the other at the peak. However, shingling the roof makes a much better-looking model and is recommended by the author.

Some Suggestions

A well-known educator once said that everyone should be able to make something with his hands of which he can be proud. If the craftsman is to be proud of the model he has made, he must make sure that all parts are carefully sanded before they are assembled as well as afterwards. The care that is taken in sanding will determine whether the model is a finished one, of which he can be proud, or otherwise. Here are a few suggestions for sanding and some general points to bear in mind:

Sandpaper with the grain of the wood and not across it.

Make a sanding block by wrapping sandpaper around three sides of a block of wood.

Emery boards are very good for sanding small pieces.

Rub small pieces of wood on the sandpaper.

Use medium and then fine sandpaper.

Smooth all edges of the completed model with fine sandpaper.

Used power-sanding belts, cut into pieces, make very good material for sanding. A fine belt is best.

To sand concave surfaces, wrap a piece of sandpaper around a dowel that is a little smaller than the curve to be sanded.

When two like pieces are needed, such as for the ends of a desk, put them in the vise, after they have been sawed out, and finish with a file and sandpaper.

Throughout the book, *pc* stands for *piece.*

Use the try square when marking on wood to assure straight lines.

Wire can be made flat by pounding it with a hammer.

Read the instructions all the way through before starting to build a model.

The size of the drill to use will depend on the size of the wire being used and may be different from the drill suggested.

The modelmaker may want to leave one side of the roof only partly covered so as to be able to look inside the building.

When two pieces of wood are to be glued together, spread a thin layer of glue on one of the pieces. Do not use too much glue; a little is better than a lot. Press the pieces firmly together. Some parts can be held together with rubber bands or with weights until the glue has set. One of the white glues is excellent for making models, such as Elmer's glue.

Finishing the Models

The models, unless otherwise suggested, may be stained and then lacquered, shellacked or varnished. Or they may be left natural as the wood will color with age. If left natural, however, it is a good idea to apply two or three coats of a clear finish. Such finishes can be applied with a small brush, or they are available in spray cans at paint or hobby stores. If a weather-beaten appearance is desired for the buildings or bridges, stains may be used to get that effect.

Special paints are manufactured for finishing models and can be purchased at a hobby store. Parts of some models, such as the spokes in the surrey wheels, can be colored with a marking pen.

In the House

Two Old Tables

A trestle table was one of the most common pieces of furniture in the early seventeenth century home. These tables, measuring some four to six feet in length, were usually made of pine or with a pine top and an understructure of hard wood. The top was made from two wide boards with cleats at each end and with two trestles to support it. The trestles were connected by a flat stretcher between the uprights. Most of the tables, often heavy and crude, were homemade in country and frontier areas.

Another piece of furniture was the hutch table, which served as a table, chair, or settle. There was also space beneath the seat, which was used as a storage compartment. The table top was held in place by wooden pegs and could be tipped down to form a table or raised to serve as the back of a chair or settle.

A Trestle Table and Benches

Materials for table:

2 pc $\frac{1}{4}''$ x $\frac{7}{8}''$ x $4\frac{1}{2}''$—top
2 pc $\frac{1}{8}''$ x $\frac{1}{4}''$ x $1\frac{3}{4}''$—cleats
2 pc $\frac{1}{4}''$ x $\frac{7}{8}''$ x $1''$—upright ⎱
2 pc $\frac{1}{4}''$ x $\frac{3}{8}''$ x $1\frac{1}{2}''$—top supports ⎰ trestles
2 pc $\frac{1}{4}''$ x $\frac{3}{8}''$ x $1\frac{5}{8}''$—bottom pc or feet
1 pc $\frac{1}{8}''$ x $\frac{1}{4}''$ x $4''$—stretcher
2 round toothpicks

Construction:

1. Glue the two planks for the table top together and add the cleats at the ends of the planks.

2. Make a notch ⅛″ wide and ¼″ deep in the center of each upright piece.

3. Center and glue the upright piece on the top and bottom pieces of the trestle, rounding off the corners as shown.

4. Glue the completed trestles to the underside of the top ½″ in from the ends.

5. Insert the stretcher through the notches allowing it to extend about ¼″ at each end. Mark the position of holes for pegs, remove stretcher, and drill holes for toothpick pegs. Replace the stretcher and insert short pieces of toothpicks into each hole.

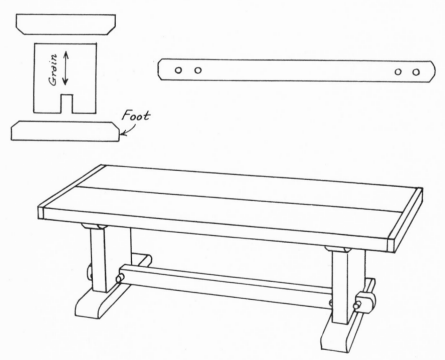

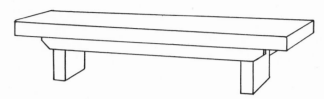

The Benches

Materials for benches:

2 pc ¼″ x ¾″ x 4″—seat
4 pc ¼″ x ½″ x ¾″—legs
4 pc ⅟₁₆″ x ¼″ x 3″—braces

Construction:

1. Glue the legs to the underside of the seat ⅝″ in from either end.

2. Glue the braces to the legs.

A Hutch Table, Settle, and Chest

Materials:

2 pc ³⁄₁₆″ x 1″ x 1½″—ends of settle
1 pc ³⁄₁₆″ x ¾″ x 2¼″—bottom ⎫
2 pc ⅛″ x ¾″ x ⁹⁄₁₆″—ends ⎬ chest
2 pc ⅟₁₆″ x ¾″ x 2¼″—sides ⎭
1 pc ⅛″ x 1″ x 2¼″ ⎫
2 pc ⅟₁₆″ x ³⁄₁₆″ x ¾″—A ⎬ seat
2 pc ⅛″ x 1¼″ x 3⅜″ ⎫
2 pc ⅛″ x ⅛″ x 2½″—end cleats ⎬ table top
2 pc ³⁄₁₆″ x ⅜″ x 2″—cross braces
1 round toothpick

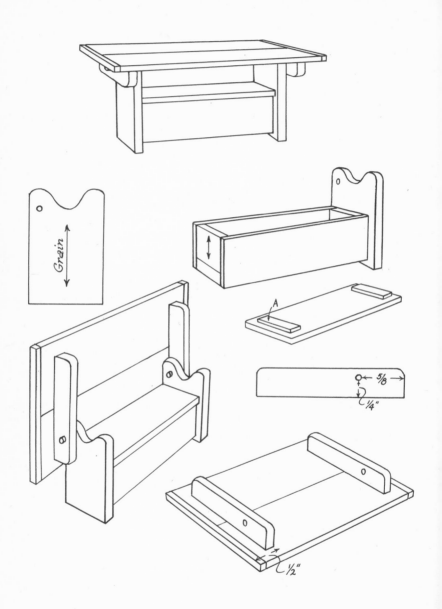

Grain

A

5/8

1/4"

1/2"

Construction:

1. Prepare the ends for the settle as shown. Drill a hole for a toothpick dowel ¼" down from the upper edge and ⅛" in from the back edge. It is a good idea to drill the two pieces together before shaping them.

2. Make the chest by gluing the ends to the bottom and then adding the sides.

3. Glue the chest between the ends ⅛" up from the lower edge and even with the back edges of the ends.

4. Fasten the A pieces to the underside of the seat ⅛" in from the ends and sides.

5. Drill a hole for a toothpick dowel in each cross brace ⅝" from one end and ¼" from one side edge. Round off the corners as shown in the diagram.

6. Glue the table top sections together and fasten the cleats to the ends.

7. Draw light lines on the underside of the table top ½" in from either end. Using these lines as guides, glue the cross braces to the table top ¼" in from the side edges. Be sure that the cross braces are 2⅝" (length of settle) apart as the settle will fit in between the braces. (The braces will be ⁵⁄₁₆" in from either end.)

8. Put the dowels through the braces and holes in ends of settle. The top should swing back easily on the dowels. If it does not, round off the back corners of the ends of the settle a little more.

Bedsteads in Colonial America

In colonial America a bedstead consisted of a frame strung with rope on which was placed a mattress filled with corn husks, leaves, or straw. As feathers became available, they were used as filling to make a featherbed. Many of the bedsteads had no footboard and a low headboard. Some frames were hinged to allow them to be folded against the wall in order to conserve space when not in use.

As the colonists and their descendants became more prosperous, four-posted bedsteads became more common. The posts were often connected at the top by a frame called a tester. The tester was covered with fabric, and many had curtains so that the bedstead could be entirely enclosed. On a cold winter night in New England, the drawn curtains helped to keep the occupants warm.

The trundle bed was designed to fit underneath the large bedstead. At night it was pulled out and used by the smaller children.

Another was known as the bundling bed, which was similar to any other bedstead except that there was sometimes a board running lengthwise between the headboard and footboard. The practice of bundling, or courting in bed, was common in the Old World and, as with many other customs, was brought to America by the immigrants. In earlier times it was condoned due to conditions that then existed. The houses were small, and young people could have more privacy while reclining in bed. It also saved firewood, and although wood was plentiful, it did have to be cut. One Connecticut clergyman once stated, "Bundling has prevailed one hundred sixty years in New England." He also said, "It is certainly innocent, virtuous and prudent, or the Puritans would not have permitted it to prevail among their offspring." Bundling, however, was not confined to New England and appears to have been common in many other parts of the New World.

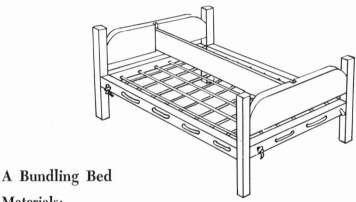

A Bundling Bed

Materials:

> 2 pc ¼″ x ¼″ x 4½″—side rails
> 2 pc ¼″ x ¼″ x 3″—end rails
> 4 pc ¼″ x ¼″ x 2½″—posts
> 2 pc ³⁄₁₆″ x ¾″ x 3″—headboard, footboard
> 1 pc ¹⁄₁₆″ x ½″ x 4¾″—divider board
> String for roping the bed

Construction:

1. Drill no. 60 holes in the side and end rails. The first hole is ¼″ in from the end of the rail and the holes are ½″ apart.

2. Draw a light line on one side of each post 1″ from the lower end.

3. Shape the headboard and footboard as in the drawings, or leave them straight. With a file make a shallow groove down through the center of each board for the divider.

4. Using the lines drawn on the posts as guides, glue the end rails to the posts 1″ up from the lower end. Glue the headboard and footboard between the posts ¼″ above the rails.

5. Glue the side rails to one end assembly, and when the glue has set, glue the other end assembly to the side rails.

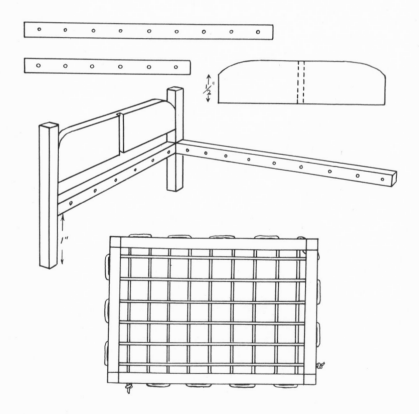

6. The old beds had rope strung back and forth between the rails to support the mattress. Beginning at the foot of the bed, tie a knot in the end of the "rope" being used to cord the bed. Make the knot large enough so that it cannot be pulled through the hole. Insert the rope through the corner hole in the rail at the foot of the bed. Carry it lengthwise of the bed through the opposite hole in the head rail. Then go on to the next hole in the head rail, back to the foot rail, and so on. When all of the lengthwise ropes have been put in, pass the rope inside one post and underneath the rail. Thread it through the first hole of the side rail and proceed as before. When completed, tie the end of the rope to keep it taut.

7. Press the divider board into the grooves.

A Tester Bed

Materials:

2 pc ¼″ x ¼″ x 4½″—side rails
2 pc ¼″ x ¼″ x 3″—end rails
4 pc ¼″ x ¼″ x 5″—posts
1 pc ³⁄₁₆″ x 1½″ x 3″—headboard
2 pc ¹⁄₁₆″ x ¼″ x 5″ ⎫
5 pc ¹⁄₁₆″ x ¼″ x 3½″ ⎬ tester frame
                              ⎭

Construction:

1. Drill no. 60 holes in the side and end rails. Start the first hole ¼″ in from one end and space the holes ½″ apart.

2. Draw a light line on one side of each post 1¼″ from the lower end. Using these lines as guides, glue the end

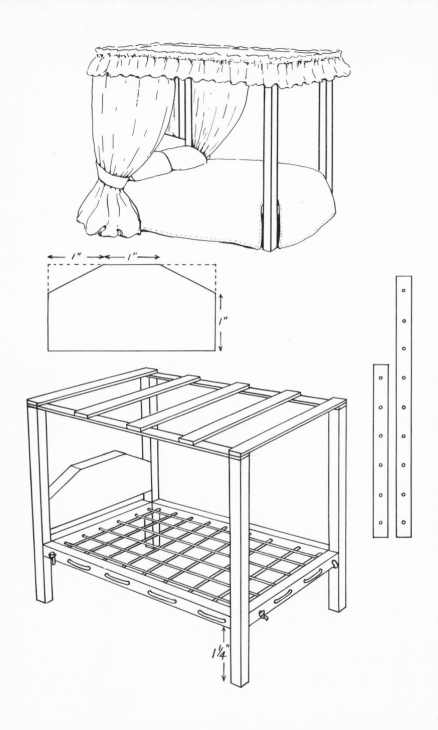

6. The old beds had rope strung back and forth between the rails to support the mattress. Beginning at the foot of the bed, tie a knot in the end of the "rope" being used to cord the bed. Make the knot large enough so that it cannot be pulled through the hole. Insert the rope through the corner hole in the rail at the foot of the bed. Carry it lengthwise of the bed through the opposite hole in the head rail. Then go on to the next hole in the head rail, back to the foot rail, and so on. When all of the lengthwise ropes have been put in, pass the rope inside one post and underneath the rail. Thread it through the first hole of the side rail and proceed as before. When completed, tie the end of the rope to keep it taut.

7. Press the divider board into the grooves.

A Tester Bed

Materials:

2 pc $\frac{1}{4}''$ x $\frac{1}{4}''$ x $4\frac{1}{2}''$—side rails
2 pc $\frac{1}{4}''$ x $\frac{1}{4}''$ x $3''$—end rails
4 pc $\frac{1}{4}''$ x $\frac{1}{4}''$ x $5''$—posts
1 pc $\frac{3}{16}''$ x $1\frac{1}{2}''$ x $3''$—headboard
2 pc $\frac{1}{16}''$ x $\frac{1}{4}''$ x $5''$ }
5 pc $\frac{1}{16}''$ x $\frac{1}{4}''$ x $3\frac{1}{2}''$ } tester frame

Construction:

1. Drill no. 60 holes in the side and end rails. Start the first hole $\frac{1}{4}''$ in from one end and space the holes $\frac{1}{2}''$ apart.

2. Draw a light line on one side of each post $1\frac{1}{4}''$ from the lower end. Using these lines as guides, glue the end

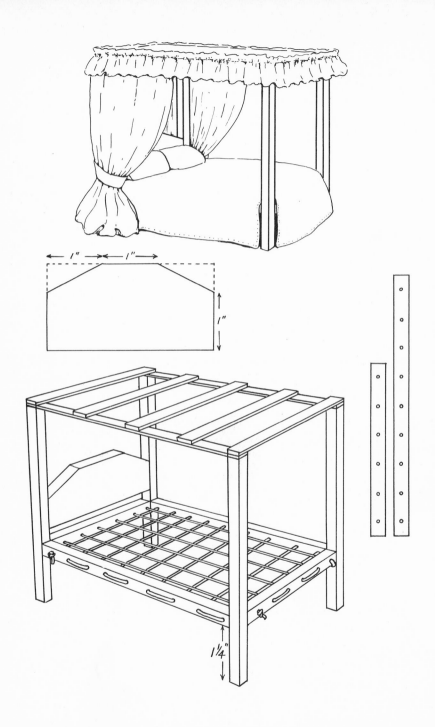

1" 1"

1"

1¼"

rails to the posts. The upper surface of the rails will be
1½″ above the floor.

3. Glue the side rails to one end assembly.

4. When the glue has set, glue the other end assembly
to the side rails.

5. Make the headboard and glue in place between the
posts ¼″ above the end rail.

6. Assemble the tester frame by gluing the longer pieces
to the upper ends of the posts and then gluing the crosspieces to them.

7. Directions for roping are the same as for the Bundling
Bed. (See page 31.)

8. Make the covering for the canopy by cutting a piece
of material about 4¾″ wide and 5¾″ long. Place it over the
frame, creasing the material along the edges.

9. For a curtain to cover the head of the bed and to extend about 2½″ along each side, cut a piece of material
about 5½″ by 16½″. Hem the edges. Gather the top edge
and sew it to the canopy covering. Use narrow strips of
hemmed material for tiebacks to go around headposts and
through an opening made in the curtain near the posts.

10. Cut a piece of material 1½″ wide and about 1¼
yards long for the valance to go around the upper edge of
the canopy frame. Hem and gather and sew to the covering
around the top edge of the frame.

11. Cut a piece of material 4¾″ wide and 6½″ long for
the mattress. Fold material in half lengthwise, with right
sides inside and edges together. Sew along one end and
side. Turn right side out and fill with cotton or other
material. Fold in the open end and sew together. Make the

pillows the same way with two pieces of material 1¼″
wide by 1½″ long.

12. Make the covering for the bed from a piece of
material about 6½″ wide and 7½″ long. Make cuts to fit
around footposts and hem edges.

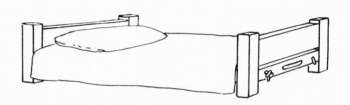

A Trundle Bed

Materials:

2 pc ¼″ x ¼″ x 3½″—side rails
2 pc ¼″ x ¼″ x 2″—end rails
4 pc ¼″ x ¼″ x 1″—posts
2 pc ³⁄₁₆″ x ⅜″ x 2″—footboard and headboard

Construction:

1. Drill seven holes in each side rail and four holes in
each end rail with a no. 60 drill. Start the first hole ¼″ in
from one end and space the holes ½″ apart.

2. Draw a light line on one side of each end post ¼″
from one end. Glue the end rails to the posts, using these
lines as guides.

3. Glue the side rails to one end assembly, and when the glue has set, glue the other end assembly to the side rails.

4. Glue the head and footboards in between the posts.

5. Directions for roping are the same as for the Bundling Bed. (See page 31.)

6. Make the mattress for the trundle bed from material 2¼" wide by 3⅝" long. See directions for the Tester Bed (page 33).

7. Use a piece of material 1¼" wide by 1½" long for the pillow, and a piece 3¾" wide by 4¼" long for the covering.

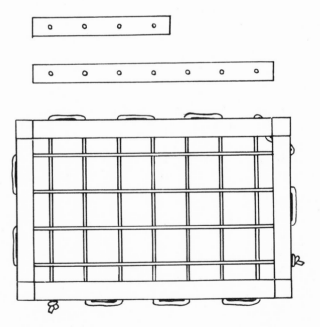

Two Old-Time Cradles

One of the most common and essential pieces of furniture to be found in the sparsely furnished home in colonial times was a cradle. These sturdily built baby beds usually had a small occupant in them.

Babies of the rich and poor alike have been rocked for hundreds of years in all types of cradles from boxlike affairs to more ornate creations. However, they all had rockers or were suspended from posts so that the baby could be rocked back and forth.

Few cradles are now made with rockers, and baby can no longer be rocked to sleep. Some doctors believe that this is not a good thing and that twentieth century babies would be better off if they could be rocked by their mothers. The old-time cradle is more often used today as a magazine rack or a place for plants rather than for the purpose for which it was made—namely, that the baby could be gently rocked to sleep.

A Swinging Cradle

Materials:

2 pc $\frac{1}{8}$" x $\frac{1}{2}$" x $1\frac{3}{4}$"—upright posts
4 pc $\frac{1}{8}$" x $\frac{1}{4}$" x $\frac{3}{4}$"—A $\Big\}$ feet
4 pc $\frac{1}{16}$" x $\frac{1}{4}$" x 2"—B
1 pc $\frac{1}{8}$" x $\frac{1}{2}$" x $2\frac{13}{16}$"—brace
2 pc $\frac{1}{8}$" x $1\frac{1}{8}$" x $\frac{7}{8}$"—ends $\Big\}$
1 pc $\frac{1}{8}$" x $\frac{7}{8}$" x $2\frac{1}{2}$"—bottom $\Big\}$ cradle
2 pc $\frac{1}{16}$" x $\frac{3}{4}$" x $2\frac{3}{4}$"—sides $\Big\}$
1 round toothpick

Construction:

1. Round off the corners of one end of each upright post. Drill a hole for a toothpick peg ¼″ from this end and centered between the side edges.

2. Make the supports for the cradle by gluing an A piece to one end of a B piece. Then attach the post, another A piece, and lastly another B piece.

3. Fasten the brace between the upright posts and on the inner B piece of the feet.

4. Shape the ends of the crib and drill a hole for a toothpick peg in each end ¼″ from the rounded edge and in the center of the piece.

5. Fasten the ends to the bottom and add the side pieces.

6. Hang the cradle with pegs cut from the toothpick.

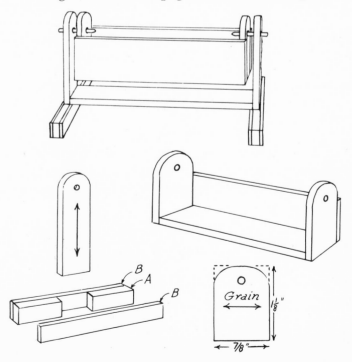

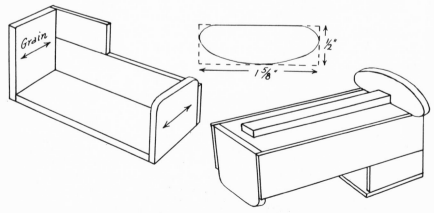

A Rocking Cradle

Materials:

1 pc ⅛″ x 1″ x 1″—end, foot
1 pc ⅛″ x 1¼″ x 1″—end, head
1 pc ⅛″ x 1″ x 2½″—bottom
2 pc ¹⁄₁₆″ x ¾″ x 2¾″ ⎤
2 pc ¹⁄₁₆″ x ½″ x 1″ ⎦ sides
1 pc ¹⁄₁₆″ x 1⅛″ x 1⅛″—top
2 pc ⅛″ x ½″ x 1⅝″—for rockers
1 pc ⅛″ x ¼″ x 2¼″—brace between rockers

Construction:

1. Round off the corners of the foot piece and glue the end pieces to the bottom.

2. Glue the longer side pieces to the ends and bottom, and then glue the shorter side pieces to the head and lower side pieces.

3. Glue on the top.

4. Center and glue the brace on the underside of the bottom and in ¼″ from each end.

5. Glue the rockers to the bottom and ends of the brace.

A Pine Cupboard

One piece of furniture often found in the seventeenth century home was a cupboard. There were many different styles, but they were all designed for the storage of dishes, tableware, pewter, and the like. In America, cupboards were often made from pine. Other woods used were chestnut, oak, poplar, and walnut.

A Pine Cupboard

Materials:

2 pc ⅛″ x ½″ x 3½″ ⎱ ends
2 pc ⅛″ x ½″ x 1½″ ⎰ ends

1 pc ⅛″ x ¾″ x 2¾″—A ⎱ top
1 pc ¹⁄₁₆″ x ½″ x 2½″—B ⎰ top

1 pc ⅛″ x 1⅛″ x 2¾″—C ⎱ bottom
1 pc ¹⁄₁₆″ x 1″ x 2½″—D ⎰ bottom

1 pc $\frac{1}{16}''$ x $2\frac{3}{4}''$ x $3\frac{3}{4}''$—back
1 pc $\frac{1}{8}''$ x $\frac{5}{8}''$ x $2\frac{3}{4}''$—E ⎫
1 pc $\frac{1}{8}''$ x $\frac{1}{2}''$ x $2\frac{1}{2}''$—F ⎬ counter top
1 pc $\frac{1}{16}''$ x $1''$ x $2\frac{1}{2}''$—G ⎭
2 pc $\frac{1}{16}''$ x $\frac{1}{2}''$ x $2\frac{1}{2}''$—upper shelves
1 pc $\frac{1}{16}''$ x $\frac{7}{8}''$ x $2\frac{1}{2}''$—bottom shelf
2 pc $\frac{3}{32}''$ x $\frac{7}{8}''$ x $1\frac{1}{2}''$—front, lower part
1 pc $\frac{3}{32}''$ x $1''$ x $1\frac{3}{8}''$—door
2 pc $\frac{1}{16}''$ x $\frac{3}{32}''$ x $1''$—door hangers
1 paper clip or pin for hinges
1 pc round toothpick—for doorknob

Construction:

1. Glue the shorter end pieces to one edge of the longer pieces. See the diagram.

2. Round off the front corners of the A piece and glue the B piece to it even with the back edge and $\frac{1}{8}''$ in from the ends of A.

3. Fasten the D piece to the C piece so that the back edges are even and it is in $\frac{1}{8}''$ from the ends of C.

4. Make the counter top by gluing the F piece to one edge of the E piece, allowing the E piece to extend $\frac{1}{8}''$ at each end. Complete the counter top by gluing the G piece to one side of the other two and even with the back edge and ends of the F piece.

5. Draw light lines on the inside of the end sections $\frac{5}{8}''$, $1\frac{1}{4}''$, and $2\frac{3}{4}''$ down from the upper end to locate the position of the shelves.

6. Assemble the cupboard by gluing the ends to the top and bottom and then putting on the back.

7. Install the shelves.

8. Put on the two front pieces, leaving an opening 1″ wide in the center for the door.

9. Drill holes in each door hanger $\frac{1}{16}″$ in from one end. Also drill holes in the upper and lower ends of the door $\frac{1}{16}″$ in from one edge and $\frac{1}{8}″$ in depth.

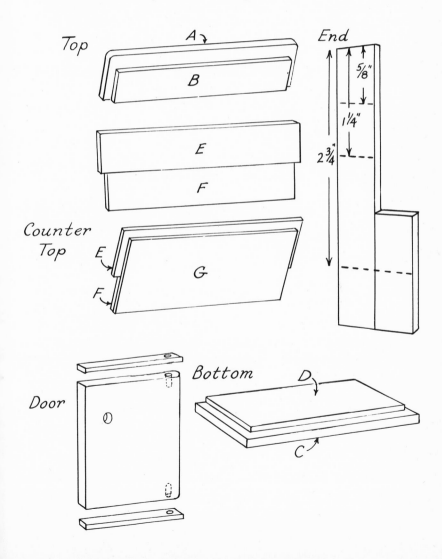

10. Glue one hanger to the bottom, between the two front pieces in the opening left for the door, with the hole to the right as you face the cupboard and against the front edge of the D piece.

11. Set the counter top temporarily in place and glue the upper hanger to the underside of the counter top against the edge of the G piece, with the hole in line with the hole in the lower hanger.

12. Drill a hole in the door about $\frac{3}{8}''$ down from the upper end for the toothpick doorknob.

13. Insert a piece of wire or pin about $\frac{3}{16}''$ long in the lower hole and set the door on it. Also insert a piece of wire or pin in the hole made in the upper end of the door. Set the counter top in place with the hole in the upper door hanger over the wire. It will no doubt be necessary to round off the edges of the door on the side of the hinges. After the door is fitted satisfactorily, glue the counter top in place.

Two Churns

During the eighteenth century, butter was made in the home in a variety of churns. The most common one was the dash churn, which was to be found in many kitchens. Another type was the rocking churn, which was a wooden box set on rockers that could be rocked either by the handles or with the foot. A later churn had paddles that were rotated by a crank.

The milk was stored in shallow containers until the cream rose to the surface. The cream was skimmed off and put into the churn. The beating, rocking, or rotation of the paddles caused the butter "to come." It was then worked to remove the remaining liquid, salted, and made into prints or shaped in molds. The liquid that was left in the churn was called buttermilk and used by many housewives in the making of pancakes.

A Rocker Churn

Materials:

2 pc $\frac{1}{8}''$ x $\frac{3}{4}''$ x $\frac{3}{4}''$—ends
2 pc $\frac{1}{16}''$ x $\frac{3}{4}''$ x 2''—sides
1 pc $\frac{1}{16}''$ x $\frac{7}{8}''$ x 2''—bottom
2 pc $\frac{1}{16}''$ x $\frac{7}{8}''$ x $\frac{3}{4}''$—top
1 pc $\frac{1}{16}''$ x $\frac{7}{8}''$ x $\frac{1}{2}''$—A ⎤
1 pc $\frac{1}{16}''$ x $\frac{7}{8}''$ x $\frac{3}{4}''$—B ⎬ cover
1 pc $\frac{1}{16}''$ x $\frac{1}{8}''$ x $\frac{1}{2}''$—handle ⎦
4 pc $\frac{1}{8}''$ x $\frac{1}{8}''$ x $\frac{7}{8}''$—cross braces
4 pc $\frac{1}{8}''$ x $\frac{1}{8}''$ x $2\frac{1}{2}''$—legs
2 pc $\frac{1}{8}''$ x $\frac{5}{8}''$ x 3''—for rockers
1 pc round toothpick—plug

Construction:

1. Glue the sides to the ends. Drill a hole for the toothpick plug in the center of the bottom and fasten on the bottom and two top pieces.

2. Glue the cross braces to the tub ⅛″ in from each end.

3. Make the cover by centering piece A on piece B and gluing it fast. Put the handle in the center of the B piece.

4. Shape the upper end of each leg piece to make a round handle.

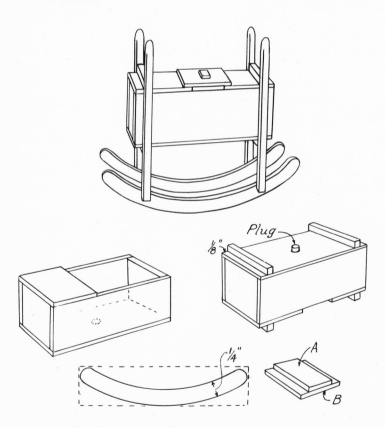

5. Glue the legs to the sides of the tub and ends of the cross braces. Each leg should extend 1″ below the bottom of the tub.

6. Cut out the rockers as in the drawing, using a small round plate to get the curve.

7. Glue the rockers to the inside of the legs.

8. Cut off a short piece of toothpick for the plug.

A Paddle Churn

Materials:

> 2 pc ⅛″ x 1″ x 1⅛″—ends of tub
> 1 pc ⅟₃₂″ x 1½″ x 3″—covering for tub (balsa wood is very good for this)
> 2 pc ⅛″ x ¼″ x 1¼″—tub crosspieces
> 2 pc ⅛″ x 1¼″ x 2½″—ends of churn
> 1 pc ⅛″ x 1″ x 1½″—cover
> 1 pc ⅟₁₆″ x ⅛″ x ¾″—handle
> 1 pc ⅛″ dowel 2″ long—shaft
> 4 pc ⅟₁₆″ x ¼″ x ¾″—ends ⎫
> 4 pc ⅟₃₂″ x ¼″ x 1⅛″—blades ⎭ paddle
> 1 pc ⅛″ x ¼″ x ⅞″ ⎫
> 1 pc round toothpick ½″ long ⎭ crank

Construction:

1. Shape the ends for the tub as shown and drill a ⁹⁄₆₄″ hole, or enlarge a ⅛″ hole slightly, in the center of each end ⅝″ down from the top. Glue the two crosspieces between the ends.

2. Glue the covering to one cross brace and the ends. When set, soak the covering in water and bend around the

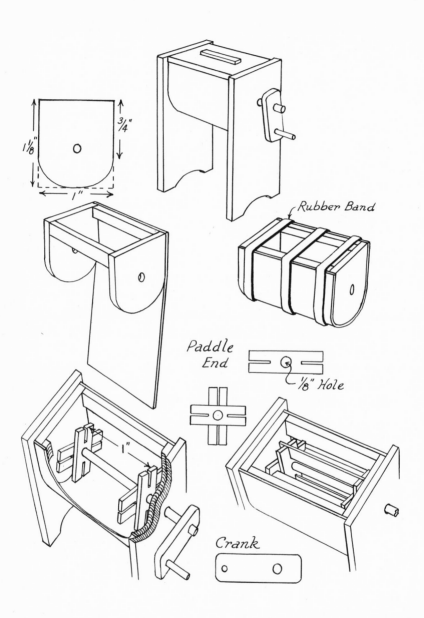

$\frac{3}{4}$"

$1\frac{1}{8}$"

1"

Rubber Band

Paddle
End

$\frac{1}{8}$" Hole

1"

Crank

ends. Hold in place with rubber bands until dry, and then glue the covering to the ends and other crosspiece.

3. Using a half-round file, shape the ends of the churn as shown. Drill a $\frac{9}{64}''$ hole in the center of each end $\frac{3}{4}''$ down from the top edge.

4. Glue the tub between the ends $\frac{1}{8}''$ down from the upper edge of the ends and $\frac{1}{8}''$ in from each side edge so that the holes coincide.

5. Make the four ends for the paddle as shown and glue together to make two crosses.

6. Insert the dowel shaft through one end of the churn, through the paddle end sections, and on through the other end. Space the paddle end sections about $1''$ apart.

7. Set the blades into the cuts made for them. (The paddle will have to be assembled inside the churn.)

8. Make the crank and put it on the end of the shaft.

9. Glue the handle to the center of the lid or cover.

Two Early American Chests

Homemade chests were the first storage places for clothing and household linens in the early colonial period. Many of these old chests were made of pine and decorated by their builders in various ways. Some of the popular designs made on the front of the crude chests were diamond-shaped and heart-shaped. Others put their initials and the date on their handiwork.

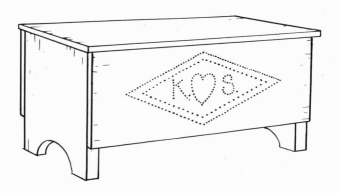

A Blanket Chest

Materials:

2 pc ⅛″ x 1¼″ x 1¾″—ends
1 pc ⅛″ x 1¼″ x 2¾″—bottom
2 pc ¹⁄₁₆″ x 1¼″ x 3″—sides
1 pc ¹⁄₁₆″ x 1½″ x 3⅛″—A ⎫
1 pc ¹⁄₁₆″ x 1¼″ x 2¾″—B ⎭ lid

Construction:

1. Using the diagram as a guide, prepare the end sections. The curved line can be made by using a five-cent piece to draw around.

2. If the front side is to be decorated, it is best to do so before attaching the sides to the ends. Outline the design on wood with a pencil and punch shallow holes with a small nail or large pin.

3. Glue the bottom between the ends ½″ up from the lower edge of the end pieces, and fasten the sides to the ends and bottom.

4. Make the lid by centering the B piece on the A piece. The A piece will extend ³⁄₁₆″ at each end and ⅛″ at each side.

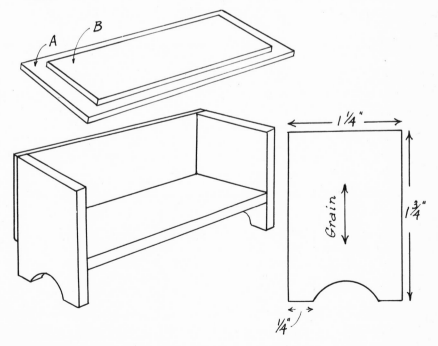

A Six-Board Chest

Materials:

2 pc ⅛″ x 1⅜″ x 1¼″—ends
2 pc ¹⁄₁₆″ x 1⅜″ x 2¾″—sides
1 pc ¹⁄₁₆″ x 1½″ x 2⅞″—A ⎫
1 pc ¹⁄₁₆″ x 1¼″ x 2½″—B ⎬ lid
1 pc ¹⁄₁₆″ x 1⅜″ x 2¾″—bottom

Construction:

1. Glue the sides to the ends and attach the bottom piece.

2. Center the B piece on the underside of the A piece, which will extend ³⁄₁₆″ at the ends and ⅛″ at the sides.

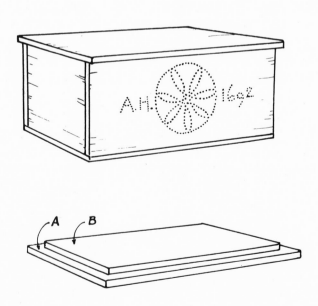

At Meetinghouse
and School

A Meetinghouse

The first houses of worship in the New World were made of logs and served as places for meetings other than religious services. They were called meetinghouses, and the people worshiped in them as well. These buildings often had dirt or sanded floors, and the people sat on hard, crude benches. There was no fireplace or chimney, as the meetinghouses were unheated. Many of them were still without a source of heat even into the first part of the nineteenth century.

As time went on, the log buildings were replaced by little clapboarded structures with raftered walls, some pews, benches, and a pulpit. The pulpit was usually a high desk, which stood on a platform at one end of the meetinghouse.

The pulpits and pews for the meetinghouse and the furniture for the schoolhouse are made to a larger scale and are not designed to fit in the buildings.

The Meetinghouse

Materials for main building:

2 pc ⅛" x 3" x 4"—ends
2 pc ¹⁄₁₆" x 1¾" x 5"—sides
1 pc ¼" x 4" x 4¾"—floor
2 pc ¼" x ¼" x 4¾"—braces
16 pc ¹⁄₁₆" x ¼" x 5¼"—roof boards
1 pc ¾" x ¾" x 1½"—steeple

1 pc $\frac{1}{8}$" x 1" x $1\frac{1}{2}$"—door
1 pc $\frac{1}{16}$" x $\frac{1}{8}$" x 1"—lower support
1 pc $\frac{1}{8}$" x $\frac{1}{8}$" x 1"—upper support
1 pc $\frac{1}{8}$" x $\frac{5}{16}$" x $\frac{3}{4}$"—sill
2 pc $\frac{1}{16}$" x $\frac{1}{8}$" x $1\frac{1}{2}$"—frame
1 small nail—knob
1 paper clip—hinges
4 windows

} door assembly

Materials for vestibule:

2 pc $\frac{1}{8}$" x 2" x $2\frac{1}{2}$"—end, roof support
2 pc $\frac{1}{16}$" x $1\frac{7}{8}$" x $1\frac{1}{2}$"—sides
1 pc $\frac{1}{4}$" x 2" x $1\frac{3}{8}$"—floor
2 pc $\frac{1}{8}$" x $\frac{1}{4}$" x $1\frac{1}{2}$"—roof support posts
10 pc $\frac{1}{16}$" x $\frac{1}{4}$" x $1\frac{5}{8}$"—roof boards
1 pc $\frac{1}{8}$" x 1" x $1\frac{1}{2}$"—door
1 pc $\frac{1}{16}$" x $\frac{1}{8}$" x 1"—lower support
1 pc $\frac{1}{8}$" x $\frac{1}{8}$" x 1"—upper support
1 pc $\frac{1}{16}$" x $\frac{1}{8}$" x $\frac{3}{4}$"—sill
2 pc $\frac{1}{16}$" x $\frac{1}{8}$" x $1\frac{1}{2}$"—sides } frame
1 pc $\frac{1}{16}$" x $\frac{1}{8}$" x $1\frac{1}{4}$"—top
1 pc $\frac{1}{4}$" x $\frac{1}{4}$" x $1\frac{1}{4}$"—step
1 small nail—knob
1 paper clip—hinges
$\frac{1}{32}$" or $\frac{1}{64}$" material—for shingles

} door assembly

Construction of main building:

1. Make the two end sections as shown in the diagram. Cut a $\frac{3}{4}$" by $1\frac{3}{4}$" opening for the doorway in one end.

2. Prepare the side sections with two $\frac{3}{8}$" by $\frac{5}{8}$" open-

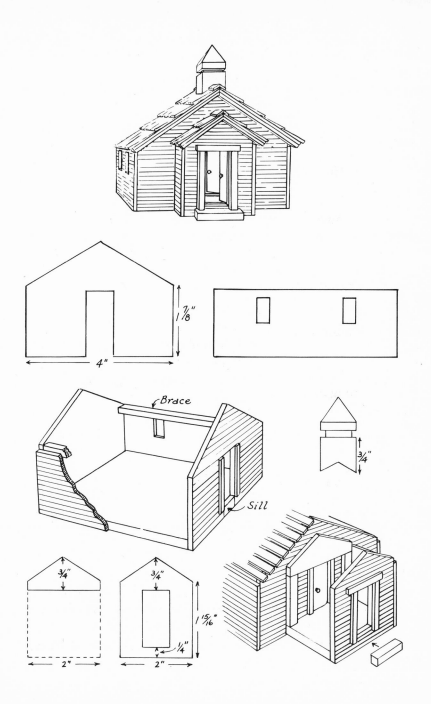

Brace

Sill

$\frac{7}{8}''$

4"

$\frac{3}{4}''$

$\frac{3}{4}''$

$\frac{3}{4}''$

$1\frac{15}{16}''$

$\frac{1}{4}''$

2"

2"

ings for the windows 1⅛" from either end and ¼" down from the upper edge.

3. Draw lines with an awl or sharp nail about ⅛" apart on the ends and sides to represent clapboard siding.

4. Glue the ends to the floor and the braces between them 1⅜" up from the floor. See the diagram.

5. Glue the sides to the floor, braces, and ends.

6. Hang the door and install the windows. See the Introduction (pages 12–14).

7. Fasten the doorsill to the end of the floor, and glue the frame pieces to each side of the doorway ¼" from the lower edge of the end.

8. Shape the steeple as shown in the diagram. Make the groove around the steeple ¾" from the end. Make a saw cut to a depth of about ⅛" and then finish with a file. The notch in the lower end must be the same angle as the roof. Glue the steeple to the roof about ½" back from the front end after the roof boards have been put on.

Construction of Vestibule:

1. Make two end sections as shown. Cut a ¾" by 1½" opening for the doorway in one end.

2. Draw lines to represent clapboards on the doorway end and the sides. Glue the end piece to the end of the floor.

3. Hang the door and set the sill in place against the lower door support.

4. Cut a ¾" piece from the peak end of the remaining end piece to make the vestibule roof support. See the diagram.

5. Center the roof support on the doorway end of the

building with the lower edge along the upper edge of the doorway and resting on the door frame. The peak should be down ½″ from the peak of the main building and in line with it.

6. Glue the supporting posts to the end of the building as shown.

7. Glue the sides to the end, posts, and floor.

8. Frame the door. Glue the step to the end of the vestibule in front of the doorway.

9. Put the roof boards on both parts of the building. Box in the ends of the boards and shingle the roof. See the Introduction (pages 15–17).

The Pulpit and Platform

Materials:

2 pc ⅛″ x 1½″ x 3″—sides
2 pc ⅛″ x 1½″ x 1½″—shelves
1 pc ¹⁄₁₆″ x 1¾″ x 3½″—front
1 pc ¹⁄₁₆″ x ½″ x 1¾″ ⎤
1 pc ¹⁄₁₆″ x 1⅛″ x 1¾″ ⎬ top
1 pc ¹⁄₁₆″ x ¹⁄₁₆″ x 1¾″ ⎦
2 pc ⅛″ x ¾″ x 5″—sides ⎤
2 pc ⅛″ x ¾″ x 3″—ends ⎬ platform
20 pc ¹⁄₁₆″ x ¼″ x 3½″—floor ⎦
1 pc ⅜″ x ¾″ x 1½″—A ⎫ steps
1 pc ⅜″ x ⅜″ x 1½″—B ⎭

Construction:

1. Prepare the side sections as shown. Locate the position of the shelves by drawing light lines ½″ up and 2″ up on inside surface of each piece.

2. Glue the shelves between the sides and put on the front.

3. Glue the two top pieces in place and fasten the narrow strip along and even with the lower edge of the wider top piece.

4. Construct the platform by gluing the ends between the sides and adding the floor boards.

5. Make the steps by gluing piece B to piece A as shown in the diagram.

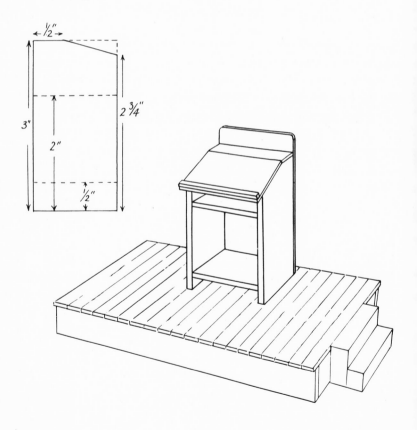

A Pew for the Meetinghouse

Materials:

2 pc ⅛″ x ¾″ x 2″—A
2 pc ⅛″ x ¾″ x 1″—B } ends
1 pc ⅛″ x ⅞″ x 3½″—seat
1 pc ¹⁄₁₆″ x 1⅛″ x 3¾″—back
2 pc ⅛″ x ¼″ x ⅜″—ends
2 pc ¹⁄₁₆″ x ⁵⁄₁₆″ x 3″—shelf and top } psalm-book rack

Construction:

1. To make the end sections glue the B pieces to the A pieces. See the diagram.

2. Fasten the ends to the back so that the top edge of the back is even with the upper edge of the ends.

3. Glue the seat in place between the ends.

4. Make the psalm-book rack by gluing the shelf and top to the ends of the end pieces. Glue the rack to the back of the pew.

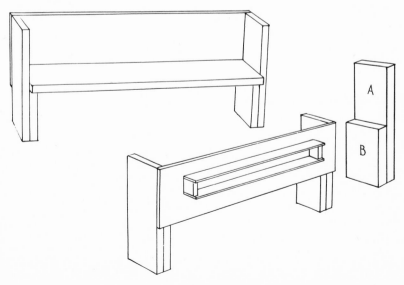

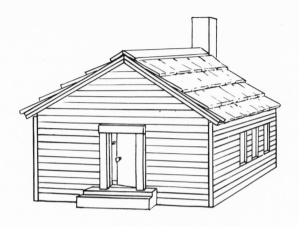

An Old District Schoolhouse

The one-room schoolhouse, once so common in our country, is fast disappearing from the American scene. District schoolhouses were built during the eighteenth and nineteenth centuries, and many were in use until well into the twentieth century.

These old-time schoolhouses were, as a rule, built near the geographical center of the district on a site that had little value for anything else. They were heated by a large fireplace or stove, with wood often provided by the parents of the pupils.

The furnishings in the schoolroom were meager, usually made by a local carpenter. In some schools the children sat on backless benches, while others had a shelf on three sides of the room with benches for the older pupils. In other schoolrooms crude desks were built for the children.

An Old District Schoolhouse

Materials:

2 pc $\frac{1}{8}''$ x $2\frac{1}{2}''$ x $3''$—ends
2 pc $\frac{1}{16}''$ x $1\frac{9}{16}''$ x $5''$—sides
1 pc $\frac{1}{4}''$ x $3''$ x $4\frac{3}{4}''$—floor
1 pc $\frac{1}{8}''$ x $2\frac{1}{4}''$ x $3''$—partition
12 pc $\frac{1}{16}''$ x $\frac{1}{4}''$ x $5\frac{1}{4}''$—roof boards
$\frac{1}{64}''$ or $\frac{1}{32}''$ material—for shingles
2 pc $\frac{1}{8}''$ x $\frac{5}{8}''$ x $1''$—doors
2 pc $\frac{1}{16}''$ x $\frac{1}{8}''$ x $\frac{5}{8}''$—bottom supports
2 pc $\frac{1}{8}''$ x $\frac{1}{8}''$ x $\frac{5}{8}''$—top supports
2 pc $\frac{1}{16}''$ x $\frac{1}{8}''$ x $1''$—sides } frame,
1 pc $\frac{1}{16}''$ x $\frac{1}{8}''$ x $\frac{7}{8}''$—top } outer door | door
1 pc $\frac{1}{16}''$ x $\frac{1}{8}''$ x $\frac{1}{2}''$—sill, outer door | assemblies
1 pc $\frac{1}{16}''$ x $\frac{3}{16}''$ x $\frac{1}{2}''$—threshold,
                   inner door
2 small nails—knobs
2 pins
1 pc $\frac{3}{8}''$ x $\frac{1}{2}''$ x $3\frac{1}{2}''$—chimney
1 pc $\frac{1}{4}''$ x $\frac{3}{8}''$ x $1\frac{1}{4}''$—A } steps
1 pc $\frac{1}{8}''$ x $\frac{1}{4}''$ x $1\frac{1}{4}''$—B } steps
12 flat toothpicks—pegs

Construction:

1. Using the drawing as a guide, make the end sections. Cut a $\frac{1}{2}''$ by $1''$ opening in the center of one end for the doorway.

2. Cut out the partition, which is $\frac{1}{4}''$ narrower than the end sections. Make the $\frac{1}{2}''$ by $1''$ doorway $\frac{1}{2}''$ from one end of the partition. Drill twelve holes $\frac{1}{4}''$ apart for pegs to hang hats and coats on. See the diagram.

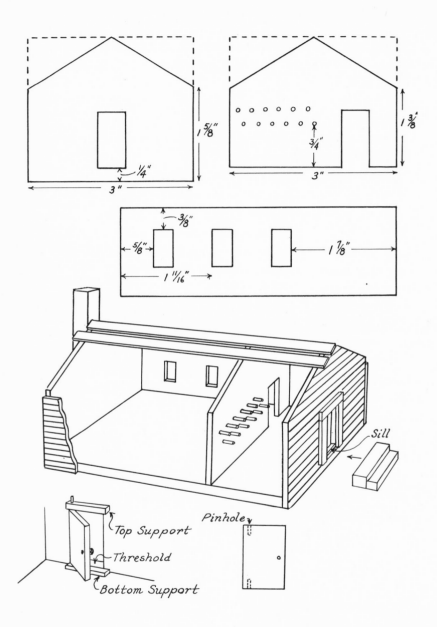

1 5/8"

3"

1/4"

1 3/8"

3/4"

3"

3/8"

5/8"

1 7/8"

1 11/16"

Sill

Top Support

Threshold

Bottom Support

Pinhole

3. Prepare the side sections. See the diagram for the location of the window openings, which are ⅝″ in height and ⅜″ in width.

4. Draw lines with an awl or nail about ⅛″ apart on the outside of the ends and sides to represent clapboard siding.

5. Glue the end sections to the ends of the floorboard.

6. Glue the sides to the ends and floor.

7. Insert short toothpick pegs into the holes in the partition. Glue the partition between the sides and to the floor 1″ from the inside of the doorway end of the building.

8. Drill a hole for the knob in each door ⅛″ from the edge, opposite the holes for the "hinges" and ⅜″ from the lower end. Hang the doors and install the windows. See the Introduction (pages 12–14).

9. Glue the doorsill against the lower door support, and glue the threshold to the floor and lower support for inside door.

10. Glue the doorframe to the sides and along the upper edge of the doorway.

11. Glue the chimney to the center of the back end of the schoolhouse.

12. Put the roof boards on, box in the ends, and shingle the roof. See the Introduction (pages 15–17).

13. Construct the steps by gluing the B piece to the A piece. Center the steps in front of the doorway and glue them to the end of the building.

Two Schoolmasters' Desks and Stools

The schoolmaster in the first schools used a table or a crude affair made by a carpenter for his desk. As time went on, more elaborate desks were provided for him. These desks had sloping tops with a hinged lid and a well or space beneath. Under the well there was usually a drawer in which could be found various articles that had been confiscated by the master.

A Desk and Platform

Materials:

> 2 pc $\frac{1}{8}$" x $1\frac{1}{2}$" x $2\frac{3}{4}$"—for sides
> 1 pc $\frac{1}{8}$" x $1\frac{1}{4}$" x $1\frac{1}{2}$"—shelf
> 1 pc $\frac{1}{8}$" x $\frac{3}{4}$" x $1\frac{1}{2}$"—bottom
> 1 pc $\frac{1}{16}$" x $1\frac{3}{4}$" x $2\frac{7}{8}$"—front
> 1 pc $\frac{1}{16}$" x $\frac{5}{8}$" x $1\frac{7}{8}$" $\Big\}$ top
> 1 pc $\frac{1}{16}$" x $1\frac{1}{8}$" x $1\frac{7}{8}$"
> 2 pc $\frac{1}{8}$" x $\frac{1}{4}$" x $\frac{1}{2}$"—ends $\Big\}$ rack
> 1 pc $\frac{1}{16}$" x $\frac{1}{4}$" x $1\frac{7}{8}$"—front
> 2 pc $\frac{1}{8}$" x $\frac{1}{4}$" x $2\frac{3}{8}$"—A $\Big\}$ frame
> 2 pc $\frac{1}{8}$" x $\frac{1}{4}$" x $1\frac{7}{8}$"—B $\Big\}$ platform
> 5 pc $\frac{1}{16}$" x $\frac{1}{2}$" x $2\frac{1}{4}$"—flooring
> 1 pc 1" dowel $\frac{1}{4}$" long—seat $\Big\}$ stool
> 3 pc $\frac{1}{8}$" dowel 2" long—legs

Construction:

1. Shape the side sections as shown in the drawings.

2. Draw a line on the inside of each side $1\frac{7}{8}$" up to locate the shelf. Glue the bottom and shelf between the sides.

3. Put on the front and top pieces.

4. Make the rack by gluing the ends to the flat top section $\frac{1}{16}''$ in from the front edge and then putting on the front piece.

5. Drill three holes in the seat of the stool at an angle so that the legs will point slightly outward.

6. Make the frame for the platform by gluing the B pieces between the A pieces and then putting on the floorboards.

7. Glue the desk and stool to the platform.

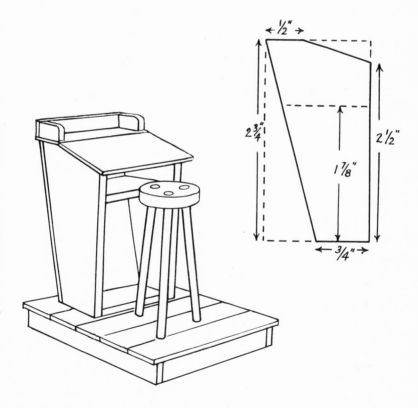

A Desk with a Drawer

Materials:

2 pc $\frac{1}{8}''$ x 1'' x $1\frac{1}{4}''$—ends

1 pc $\frac{3}{16}''$ x 1'' x $1\frac{3}{4}''$—back

1 pc $\frac{1}{8}''$ x $1\frac{1}{16}''$ x $1\frac{3}{4}''$—bottom of well

1 pc $\frac{1}{16}''$ x $1\frac{3}{8}''$ x 2''—bottom of desk

2 pc $\frac{1}{16}''$ x $\frac{3}{8}''$ x 2''—front, top

1 pc $\frac{1}{16}''$ x $\frac{1}{4}''$ x 2''—A, strip on top piece

1 pc $\frac{1}{16}''$ x 1'' x 2''—lid

1 pc $\frac{1}{16}''$ x $\frac{1}{16}''$ x 2''—B, strip on lid

4 pc $\frac{3}{16}''$ x $\frac{3}{16}''$ x $1\frac{1}{4}''$—legs

2 pc $\frac{3}{16}''$ x $\frac{3}{16}''$ x $\frac{7}{8}''$—leg spacers

1 pc $\frac{1}{8}''$ x $\frac{7}{8}''$ x $1\frac{9}{16}''$—bottom ⎫

2 pc $\frac{1}{16}''$ x $\frac{5}{16}''$ x $\frac{7}{8}''$—sides ⎪

1 pc $\frac{1}{16}''$ x $\frac{5}{16}''$ x $1\frac{11}{16}''$—back ⎬ drawer

1 pc $\frac{1}{16}''$ x $\frac{5}{16}''$ x 2''—front ⎪

1 round toothpick for knobs ⎭

1 pc $\frac{1}{4}''$ x $\frac{3}{4}''$ x 1''—seat ⎫ stool

4 pc $\frac{1}{8}''$ dowel $1\frac{1}{2}''$ long—legs ⎭

2 small paper clips—for hinges

Construction:

1. Cut out the end sections and glue them to the back piece, which will fit between the ends.

2. Glue the bottom of the desk well between the ends, against the back and $\frac{3}{8}''$ from the lower edge of the ends.

3. Glue the front piece on so that the top edge is even with the upper edges of the ends.

4. Glue the top piece to the flat part of the ends, and glue strip A to the top piece as shown.

5. Attach the bottom, which will extend ⅛″ in front.

6. Glue piece B to the lid. See the diagram.

7. Construct the drawer by gluing the side pieces to the bottom and then adding the back.

8. Drill two no. 45 holes in the front of the drawer ⅜″ from either end and midway between the top and bottom edges. Insert a short piece of toothpick into each hole for knobs.

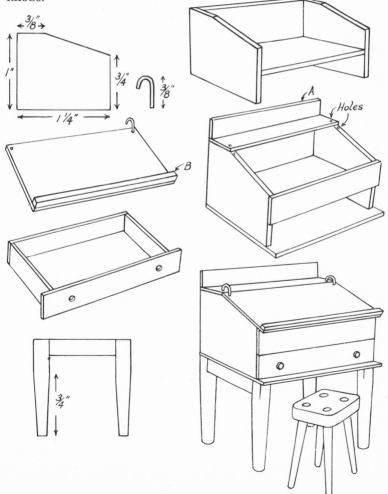

9. Glue the front piece on the drawer allowing it to extend an equal distance at each end.

10. Taper each leg at the lower end and glue a leg to each end of the spacers. Glue the leg assemblies to the underside of the desk about $\frac{1}{16}''$ in from the back and ends.

11. Use pieces cut from paper clips for hinges. Drill two small holes each $\frac{1}{16}''$ from the back edge and $\frac{1}{16}''$ from either end of the lid. Set the lid temporarily in place and mark the position of the holes on the upper edge of the ends of the desk. Drill holes about $\frac{1}{4}''$ in depth in the ends. Put the hinge in the hole and mark where the shorter end touches the flat piece on the top of the desk. Drill holes through the flat piece for these ends to set into. Attach the lid by putting the longer ends of the hinges down through the holes in the lid and into the holes in the ends of the desk.

12. Make the stool by drilling four $\frac{1}{8}''$ holes in the seat at a slight angle so that the legs will point outward. Taper the lower ends of the legs and insert them into the holes.

Pupils' Desks and a Dunce Stool

Materials:

2 pc $\frac{1}{8}''$ x $1\frac{1}{2}''$ x $1\frac{7}{8}''$—for ends

1 pc $\frac{1}{16}''$ x $^{15}\!/_{16}''$ x 2''—A ⎫
1 pc $\frac{1}{8}''$ x $\frac{1}{2}''$ x $1\frac{5}{8}''$—B ⎬ top

1 pc $\frac{1}{16}''$ x $1\frac{1}{8}''$ x 2''—back

1 pc $\frac{1}{16}''$ x $\frac{5}{8}''$ x 2''—seat

2 pc $\frac{1}{8}''$ x $\frac{1}{2}''$ x $\frac{7}{8}''$—legs ⎫
1 pc $\frac{1}{8}''$ x $\frac{1}{2}''$ x $1\frac{1}{2}''$—brace ⎬ rear seat
1 pc $\frac{1}{16}''$ x $1\frac{1}{8}''$ x 2''—back ⎪
1 pc $\frac{1}{16}''$ x $\frac{5}{8}''$ x 2''—seat ⎭

1 pc ¾" dowel ¼" long—seat ⎫
3 pc ⅛" dowel 2" long—legs ⎬ dunce stool
1 pc ⅛" x 2¼" x length needed—"floor board" ⎭

Construction:

1. Make the ends as shown in the diagrams.

2. Glue piece B to the underside of piece A ³⁄₁₆" from the ends of A and ¼" from one side edge.

3. Glue the ends to the top so that the front edge is even with the front edge of the top and against the ends of B.

4. Fasten the back in place and then the seat.

5. The last desk in the row in the old district school-house had to have a separate seat. Glue the brace to the seat ¼″ in from the ends and even with one edge (back). Glue the legs to the ends of the brace and the seat board. Fasten the back to the brace and edge of the seat.

6. Glue one or more desks and a rear seat to the "floor board."

7. Make a stool for the "dunce" similar to the one made for the schoolmaster. Drill three holes in the seat of the stool at an angle so that the legs will point slightly outward.

A Bench for Younger Children

Materials:

1 pc ⅛″ x ⅝″ x 4″—seat
3 pc ⅛″ x ½″ x ¾″—legs
2 pc ⅛″ x ½″ x 1½″—ends
2 pc ¹⁄₁₆″ x ¼″ x 4″—stretchers

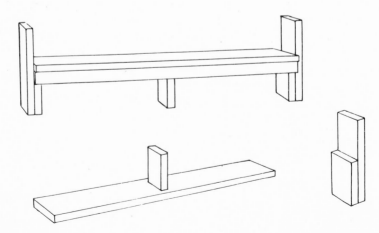

Construction:

1. Glue one leg to the center of the underside of the seat.

2. Glue each of the other legs to an end piece even with the lower edge of the end.

3. Center the seat board on the legs and glue it to them and the ends.

4. Glue the stretchers to the seat and legs.

A Bench for Older Pupils

Materials:

1 pc $\frac{1}{8}''$ x $\frac{3}{4}''$ x 4″—seat
3 pc $\frac{3}{16}''$ x $\frac{1}{2}''$ x 1″—legs
2 pc $\frac{1}{16}''$ x $\frac{1}{4}''$ x 4″—stretchers

Construction:

1. Glue one leg to the center of the underside of the seat board and the others $\frac{1}{8}''$ in from each end. The legs will also be $\frac{1}{8}''$ in from the side edges of the seat.

2. Fasten the stretchers to the seat and legs.

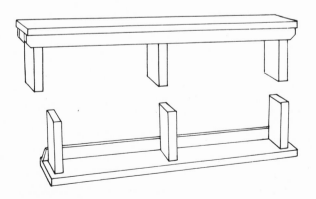

A Wood-burning Stove

Materials:

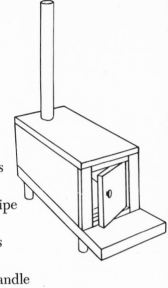

1 pc ¼″ x 1⅝″ x 3¾″—base
4 pc ³⁄₁₆″ dowel ¾″ long—legs
2 pc ⅛″ x 1½″ x 3″—sides
1 pc ¼″ x 1½″ x 1¼″—end
2 pc ¼″ x ¼″ x 1¼″—cross braces
1 pc ⅛″ x 1½″ x 3⅛″—top
1 pc ¼″ dowel 2½″ long—stovepipe
2 pc ⅛″ x ¼″ x 1½″—A
2 pc ⅛″ x ⅛″ x 1″—door supports
1 pc ⅛″ x 1″ x 1¼″—door
1 pin or round toothpick—door handle
1 paper clip

Construction:

1. Glue the sides to the end.

2. Glue the two cross braces between the sides at the opposite end. See the diagram.

3. Drill four ³⁄₁₆″ holes in the base for the legs. The holes are ¼″ from the side edges, ½″ from one end and 1″ from the other end.

4. Insert the legs into the holes.

5. Glue an A piece to the end of each side and the cross braces.

6. Glue door supports to the two cross braces. The upper support will be even with the upper edge of the brace while the lower support will be even with the lower edge of that brace.

7. Set the door temporarily in place and drill a small

hole ¼″ in depth through each support and into the door about ¹⁄₁₆″ from the ends of the supports and door.

8. Round off the inside edge of the door on the side where the holes were drilled.

9. Drill a hole in the door for the handle, which can be a piece of round toothpick or a piece cut from a pin.

10. Insert pieces of wire about ⅜″ in length through the door supports and into the holes in the door.

11. Glue the body of the stove to the base, which will extend ⅝″ at the door or front end.

12. Make a ¼″ hole ½″ from one end of the top and midway between the side edges for the stovepipe.

13. Fasten the top on the stove.

14. Paint the stove and pipe black.

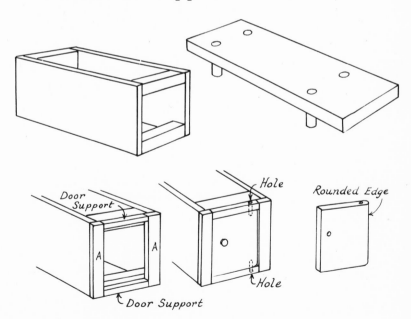

Door Support

Hole

Door Support

Hole

Rounded Edge

In the Barn

Barns—Then and Now

Various types of barns were built in America, depending on the use to which they were put and the building materials available in the area. In Pennsylvania, stone was used extensively in the construction of barns, and many old barns made partly or entirely of stone are still to be found there.

The early barns probably had a gable roof as did the tobacco barns of Connecticut. The climate and soil of the Connecticut Valley were good for the plants, and the growing of tobacco was one of the oldest means of making a living in Connecticut. The Indians grew it before the white man came, and tobacco was planted and harvested as early as 1640 in Windsor.

When grown, the tobacco plant was cut and left on the ground to wilt. It was then put on poles and hung up to dry in sheds or barns designed for that purpose.

The barns had ventilators—boards that swung outward on wooden hinges. Long hooks were used to secure the ventilators when in a closed position.

The framework for the barns was prepared and partially assembled on the ground. When all was ready, the neighbors for miles around gathered for the barn "raising." The parts of the frame were fitted together and held in place with wooden pins or trunnels.

Introduction to the Construction of Barns and Bridges

Every effort has been made to simplify the construction of the barns and bridges, yet have the finished model as realistic as possible. Due to varying thicknesses or slight differences in length or width of materials used, minor adjustments will have to be made from time to time as the model is being constructed.

Builders of earlier days fastened their barns and bridges together with mortise and tenon joints and trunnels or tree-nails. Trunnels were of different sizes, but those used for the lattice truss bridge were 1¾" to 2" in diameter. In building the models, glue takes the place of the mortise and tenon and toothpicks are the trunnels.

One brand of round toothpick (Diamond) is uniform in size and makes excellent trunnels for the bridges. Cut the toothpicks in half with a knife or razor blade. It is best to glue the parts together and then make holes with a no. 45 drill for the trunnels. Drive them through the holes, and cut off the pointed ends, allowing the trunnel to protrude slightly on each side.

Longer bridges can be made by lengthening the sides. Two types of trusses for longer bridges are shown in the drawings. One is the queen-post truss, and the other is the multiple king-post truss. The lattice truss is described in more detail, as this truss, while not difficult to construct, is somewhat more involved. However, it does make a most attractive model.

If the model builder wishes to make longer bridges than those included here, it will be necessary to lengthen the chords and other parts that run lengthwise of the bridge. More cross braces, rafters, siding, flooring, and planks will, of course, be needed, depending on the length of the bridge.

An Old Stone Barn

Materials:

2 pc ¼″ x ¼″ x 6″—A ⎤
2 pc ¼″ x ¼″ x 2½″—B ⎦ } sills

4 pc ⅛″ x ¼″ x 1½″ ⎤
2 pc ⅛″ x ¼″ x 2″ ⎦ } post spacers

8 pc ¼″ x ¼″ x 2½″—braces ⎤
8 pc ¼″ x ¼″ x 2¾″—posts ⎦ } frame sections

7 pc ⅛″ x ¼″ x 2½″—floor joists

5 pc ⅛″ x ½″ x 5½″—flooring

2 pc ¼″ x 3″ x 6″—side forms

2 pc ¼″ x 3½″ x 5″—end forms

2 pc ¼″ x ¼″ x 2½″—top, bottom ⎤
2 pc ¼″ x ¼″ x 2⅛″—sides ⎦ } doorframe

1 pc ¼″ x ⅜″ x 2″—filler

2 pc ¼″ x 1″ x 2⅛″—doors ⎤
4 pc ⅛″ x ⅛″ x ⅞″—hinges ⎥
2 pc 1⁄16″ x ⅛″ x ½″—handles ⎥ } door assembly
2 paper clips ⎦

5 pc ⅛″ x ¼″ x 3″—A

2 pc ⅛″ x ¼″ x 2⅞″—B } rafters

3 pc ⅛″ x ¼″ x 2¾″—C

6 pc 1⁄16″ x ¼″ x 2½″—braces

2 pc ⅛″ x ¼″ x 6″—plates

1 pc ¼″ x ¼″ x 2″—X, brace above doorway

8 pc ⅛″ x ¼″ x 1 13⁄32″—rafter spacers

20 pc 1⁄16″ x ¼″ x 7¼″—roof boards

4 pc 1⁄16″ x ½″ x length required ⎱ to box in ends
4 pc 1⁄16″ x ⅛″ x length required ⎰

1⁄32″ material (or 1⁄64″ if available)—for shingles

Construction:

1. Make the sills by gluing the B pieces between the A pieces. Check with the try square to make sure that the corners are square.

2. Set the floor joists in place ¾″ apart. Also glue a joist to the inside of each end sill for the flooring to rest on.

3. Draw a line across each of eight of the posts 1¼″ from one end (lower). Glue a cross brace between each of the four pairs of posts 1¼″ up, using the lines as guides to locate the brace. Fasten another brace between the posts at the upper end.

4. Glue one end frame section to the sills, then 1½″ spacers, another frame section, the 2″ spacers, then the remaining pair of 1½″ spacers and the last frame section. Make sure that the frame sections are in a straight line and perpendicular to the sills.

5. Lay the flooring.

6. Cut an opening 2″ wide and 2¼″ high in one of the side forms for the doorway.

7. Make the end forms.

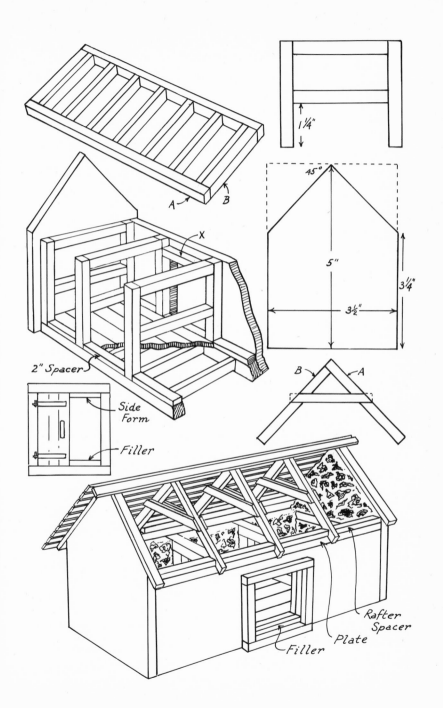

A

B

X

2" Spacer

Side
Form

Filler

45°

5"

3¼"

3½"

1¼"

B

A

Rafter
Spacer

Plate

Filler

8. Glue the side forms to the posts and sills. Fasten the end forms in place. On the inside of the form with the doorway, glue brace X between the two middle frame sections and even with the upper edge of the doorway.

9. Prepare a mixture of shredded papier-mâché and cover the inside of the barn except the floor, to a depth of $\frac{3}{16}''$ to $\frac{1}{4}''$. Fill in between the posts and braces, leaving them exposed. Press small pieces of stone into the mixture.

10. Cover the outside of the forms the same way. Before pressing pieces of stone into the ends, mark the location of the vent slits. When the material is partly set, make the slits with a blunt end tool such as a screwdriver. Use a thinner coating, or about $\frac{1}{8}''$ in depth, along the upper side edges so as not to interfere with the rafters when they are put in.

11. Make three rafter assemblies by gluing the B pieces to the A pieces and putting a brace on each side. Cut off the protruding ends of the braces. Glue the other four rafters to the gable ends of the forms, allowing the A piece to overlap the B piece at the peak. These rafters should be glued to the forms with the wider side on the forms.

12. Fasten the plates to the edges of the side forms. Glue the spacers to the plates, starting at one end, and leaving a $\frac{1}{8}''$ opening between each spacer for the rafters to fit into. Install the rafters, making sure that they are in line with the two end peaks.

13. Put on the roof boards and shingle the roof; then hang the doors. See the Introduction (pages 14–17).

Note: The construction of this barn may be simplified by leaving out the rafters and just gluing the roof boards to the end sections.

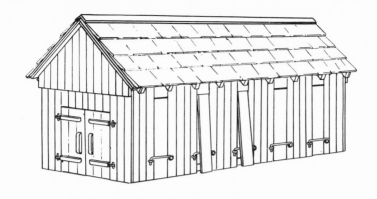

A Connecticut Tobacco Barn

Materials:

2 pc ¼″ x ¼″ x 8″—A ⎫
2 pc ¼″ x ¼″ x 2½″—B ⎭ sills

2 pc ¼″ x ¼″ x 8″—plates

23 pc ¼″ x ¼″ x 2½″—frame posts, braces

2 pc ¼″ x ¼″ x 2¼″—sides ⎫
1 pc ¼″ x ¼″ x 1⅝″—head ⎭ doorframe

59 pc ¹⁄₁₆″ x ¼″ x 2¹⁵⁄₁₆″—sides, ends ⎫

6 pc ¹⁄₁₆″ x ¼″ x ¾″ ⎫
1 pc ¹⁄₁₆″ x ⅛″ x ¾″ ⎭ above doors

26 pc ¹⁄₁₆″ x ¼″ (cut to length needed)—
gable ends ⎬ siding

10 pc ¹⁄₁₆″ x ½″ x 2¹⁷⁄₃₂″—side ventilators

10 pc ¹⁄₁₆″ x ½″ x ⅜″—siding above side ventilators

2 pc ¹⁄₁₆″ x ½″ x 2⁵⁄₃₂″—end ventilators

2 pc ¹⁄₁₆″ x ½″ x ¾″—siding above end ventilators

12 pc ¹⁄₁₆″ x ⅛″ x ¾″—hinges for ventilators

12 pc ¹⁄₁₆″ x ⅛″ x 1⅛″—hinge supports

9 pc $\frac{1}{8}''$ x $\frac{1}{4}''$ x $2\frac{5}{8}''$—A ⎫
9 pc $\frac{1}{8}''$ x $\frac{1}{4}''$ x $2\frac{3}{8}''$—B ⎭ rafters

16 pc $\frac{1}{16}''$ x $\frac{1}{4}''$ x $2''$—braces

2 pc $\frac{1}{16}''$ x $\frac{1}{4}''$ x $2\frac{5}{8}''$—X ⎫
2 pc $\frac{1}{16}''$ x $\frac{1}{4}''$ x $2\frac{3}{8}''$—Y ⎭ fillers   ⎫ rafter assembly

10 pc $\frac{1}{8}''$ x $\frac{1}{4}''$ x $\frac{7}{8}''$ ⎫
2 pc $\frac{1}{8}''$ x $\frac{1}{4}''$ x $\frac{3}{4}''$ ⎬ spacers
4 pc $\frac{1}{4}''$ x $\frac{1}{4}''$ x $\frac{7}{8}''$—ends ⎭

2 pc $\frac{1}{16}''$ x $1\frac{3}{16}''$ x $2\frac{1}{8}''$—doors ⎫
2 pc $\frac{1}{16}''$ x $\frac{1}{8}''$ x $\frac{1}{2}''$—handles ⎬ door assembly
4 pc $\frac{1}{8}''$ x $\frac{1}{8}''$ x $\frac{3}{4}''$—hinges
2 paper clips ⎭

fine wire for hooks and staples

10 pins

16 pc $\frac{1}{16}''$ x $\frac{1}{4}''$ x $8\frac{3}{4}''$—roof boards

4 pc $\frac{1}{16}$ x $\frac{1}{4}''$ x length needed ⎫
4 pc $\frac{1}{16}''$ x $\frac{1}{8}''$ x length needed ⎭ to finish gable ends

$\frac{1}{32}''$ material (or $\frac{1}{64}''$ if available)—for shingles

Construction:

1. Make the sills by gluing the B pieces (or end sills) between the A pieces. Check with the try square to make sure that the resulting rectangle has square corners.

2. Construct five frame sections by drawing a line across each of ten posts $1\frac{1}{4}''$ from one end (lower). Glue two braces between the posts, one at the upper ends and one $1\frac{1}{4}''$ up from the lower ends. The other frame section will have only one brace at the upper end and will be at the end of the barn where the doors will be located.

3. Glue the frame sections to the sill. The second one will be $1\frac{3}{8}''$ from the end section while the others are $1\frac{1}{4}''$

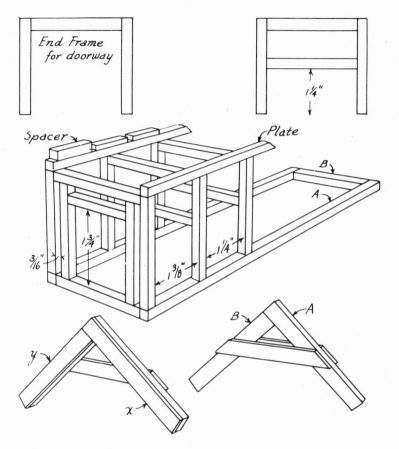

End Frame
for doorway

Spacer

Plate

B

A

$1\frac{1}{4}''$

$1\frac{3}{4}''$

$\frac{3}{16}''$

$1\frac{3}{8}''$

$1\frac{1}{4}''$

B

A

y

x

apart. Be sure that the sections are perpendicular to the sill and are in a straight line.

4. Glue the plates to the upper ends of the posts.

5. Set each of the side posts of the doorframe between the sill and brace and $\frac{3}{16}''$ in from the corner posts, leaving a $1\frac{5}{8}''$ opening for the doors. Glue the head piece between these posts $1\frac{3}{4}''$ up from the sill.

6. Make the rafter assemblies by gluing a B piece to an A piece and a cross brace on each side of seven pairs of

rafters. Put but one brace on two pairs. These will be the end rafters. Glue the filler pieces, X and Y, to the sides of the end rafters opposite the cross brace. Cut off the protruding ends of all braces even with the upper edges of the rafters.

7. Glue the end rafter spacers to the plates $\frac{1}{8}''$ in from the ends of the plates. Fasten the other spacers to the plate, using a piece of $\frac{1}{8}''$ material to space them $\frac{1}{8}''$ apart. Work in from either end of the barn with the $\frac{7}{8}''$ spacers and use the $\frac{3}{4}''$ spacers near the middle. Some slight change may have to be made in the length of these spacers due to possible varying thicknesses of the rafters.

8. Attach siding to the sides of the barn, first starting at a corner post, using boards vertically. Put on three long boards, then a short piece, then four long boards, a short piece, and so on ending with three long boards. The ends of the siding should be down $\frac{1}{16}''$ from the top of the plates and even with the bottom of the sills.

Side the closed end of the barn the same way, allowing the corner boards to overlap the edges of the first side boards. There will be only three boards between the end ventilators instead of four as on the sides.

Apply three pieces of siding to each side of the door opening and glue the short pieces above the opening.

9. Glue a hinge strip to one end of each ventilator, even with the end. The hinge will extend $\frac{1}{8}''$ at each end. Set the ventilators in position in the openings with the hinge to the inside and at the top.

10. Apply glue to the ends of the hinge supports, and set these supports against and under the hinge and across the ventilator opening. These supports will be fastened

to the inside of the siding on either side of the opening. Slide the support down leaving an opening about ⅟₃₂″ wide at the upper end of the ventilator so that it can swing outward.

11. Glue the end pairs of rafters to the ends of the spacers and the plate with the cross braces to the inside. Glue the other rafter assemblies in place, making sure that the peaks are in a straight line with the end pairs, which should be centered on the barn.

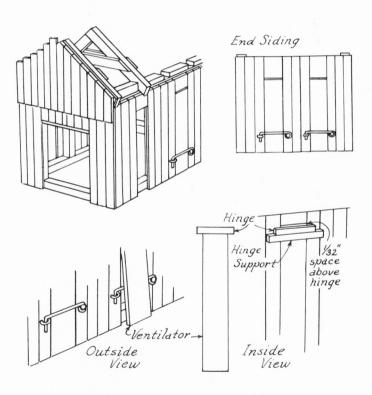

End Siding

Hinge

Hinge
Support

⅟₃₂″
space
above
hinge

Ventilator→

Outside
View

Inside
View

12. Side the gable ends by gluing pieces of siding, cut to the length needed, to the end rafters and end siding. These pieces should overlap the lower siding by about ¼″ and extend a little above the upper surface of the rafters. The protruding ends should be cut off even with the upper side of the rafters.

13. Glue the roof boards to the rafters, leaving a little space between the boards, box in the gable ends, and shingle the roof. See the Introduction (pages 15–17).

14. Hang the doors. See the Introduction (pages 14–15).

15. Make hooks about ¾″ long and small staples from fine wire to hold the ventilators either open or closed. Fasten the hooks to the siding about ¾″ up from the lower ends with pieces cut from pins.

Some Old Weathervanes

The early weathervanes, whittled from wood or hammered out of sheet iron, date from the beginning of the eighteenth century at least. Weathervanes were mounted on houses and barns for telling the direction of the wind. The first ones were simple shapes, such as an arrow, fish, or whale. Later, the designs became more complex, and all kinds of shapes were used, including cows, horses, roosters, vehicles, eagles, and the like. Factories began producing large numbers of weathervanes in the early nineteenth century.

Some Old Weathervanes

Materials:

1⁄8″ wood from which to cut vanes
1 pc 1⁄4″ x 11⁄2″ x 11⁄2″—base, A ⎤
1 pc 1⁄4″ x 1″ x 1″—base—B ⎥
1 pc 3⁄16″ dowel 2″ long—post ⎬ stand
2 pc 1⁄8″ x 1⁄4″ x 21⁄2″—crosspieces ⎦
4 paper clips—for letters
1 large pin or wire from a paper clip 11⁄2″–13⁄4″ long

Construction:

1. Saw the weathervane from the wood in the chosen shape. A short piece cut from the head of a pin makes a good eye for the fish and rooster.

2. If mounted on an arrow, saw out the arrow separately and glue the rooster to it.

3. Drill a small hole about two-fifths of the way from the front end of the vane for the pin or wire mounting to fit into. The weathervane will pivot on this pin or wire.

4. Shape the letters N,S,E,W from paper clips as shown. They may be flattened by pounding.

5. Glue the two crosspieces together to form a cross. Drill a small hole in the center for the pin or wire. Also drill the same size hole about 1⁄4″ in depth in one end of the dowel post.

6. Drill holes in the ends of the crosspieces for the letters which will rest on the crosspieces.

7. Drill a 3⁄16″ hole in the center of base piece B. Center and glue this piece on piece A. Insert the dowel post.

8. Insert pin or wire into the hole in the end of the dowel and mount the vane on it.

On the Road

Two Old Sleighs

A hundred and more years ago, the dirt roads were rough and often rutted in summer. Snow-covered in winter, they were far better for hauling loads of produce to market. The heavy winter snows made smooth highways for the many types of sleighs to be found in America. Even today, in many rural areas, these same sleighs can be seen drawn by one or two horses, often with bells jingling on the harness. One kind that was, and frequently still is, seen in Pennsylvania was called the Dutch sleigh. Some of these had two seats, while others had but one.

An Early American Sleigh
Materials:

2 pc $\frac{1}{8}''$ x $2\frac{1}{2}''$ x $3\frac{1}{2}''$—for sides
1 pc $\frac{3}{16}''$ x $2\frac{1}{2}''$ x $2\frac{1}{8}''$—back
1 pc $\frac{3}{16}''$ x $1\frac{3}{8}''$ x $2\frac{1}{8}''$—front
1 pc $\frac{3}{16}''$ x $2\frac{3}{4}''$ x $2\frac{7}{8}''$—bottom
2 pc $\frac{3}{16}''$ x $\frac{5}{8}''$ x $\frac{3}{4}''$—seat supports
1 pc $\frac{1}{8}''$ x $\frac{3}{4}''$ x $2\frac{1}{8}''$—seat
2 pc $\frac{1}{4}''$ x $1\frac{1}{4}''$ x $4''$—for runners
3 pc $\frac{1}{8}''$ x $\frac{1}{4}''$ x $2\frac{3}{4}''$—body supports
6 pc $\frac{1}{8}''$ dowel $\frac{7}{8}''$ long—upright posts
1 pc $\frac{1}{4}''$ x $\frac{1}{4}''$ x $2''$—runner cross brace
2 pc $\frac{1}{8}''$ dowel $5''$ long—shafts
2 pc $\frac{1}{8}''$ x $\frac{1}{4}''$ x $2\frac{5}{8}''$—A $\Big\}$ shaft cross brace
1 pc $\frac{1}{8}''$ x $\frac{1}{4}''$ x $2\frac{3}{8}''$—B
1 pc $\frac{1}{8}''$ x $\frac{1}{8}''$ x $2''$—singletree

Construction:

1. Cut out the sides using the drawing as a guide.
2. Round off the upper edges of the front and back ends

or leave them straight if you prefer. Glue the sides to the ends. Hold the pieces firmly with rubber bands until the glue sets.

3. Center the body assembly on the bottom and glue it.

4. Glue a seat support to each side and the bottom. Fasten the seat to the supports with glue.

5. Saw out the runners and finish with a file and sandpaper. Drill three ⅛″ holes in each runner as shown. Also drill a small hole in the curved end of each runner, ¼″ from the tip, for a pin or toothpick peg, which will attach the shafts to the runners.

6. Drill ⅛″ holes in each body support ¼″ from the ends. Insert the pieces of dowel into each hole in the runners and into the holes in the body supports.

7. Center the runner cross brace between the runners, on the two small holes, and glue it. It will be ⅛″ from the upper end of the runners.

8. Flatten one end of each shaft by squeezing it in a vise. Drill a no. 60 hole ¼″ in from the ends. Taper the opposite end with a file or sandpaper.

9. Make the shaft cross brace by gluing piece B in between the two A pieces, which will extend ⅛″ at each end of B. Drill a small hole down through the center of the assembled brace for a pin or toothpick peg.

10. Attach the shafts to the runners and runner cross brace with pins or toothpick pegs.

11. Insert the shaft cross brace between the shafts so that it is about ¾″ in front of the runners. Glue and hold in place with rubber bands until the glue sets.

12. Shape the singletree and fasten it to the shaft cross brace with a pin or peg through the center hole.

13. Center the body on the body supports and glue it.

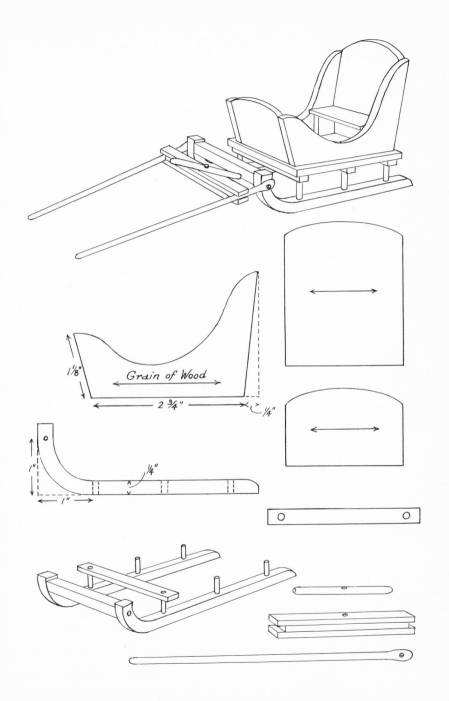

Grain of Wood

1⅛"

2 ¾"

¼"

1"

¼"

1"

A Dutch Sleigh

Materials:

2 pc $\frac{3}{16}''$ x $\frac{3}{4}''$ x 2''—ends ⎫
2 pc $\frac{1}{16}''$ x $\frac{3}{4}''$ x 4''—sides ⎬ box
1 pc $\frac{1}{16}''$ x $2\frac{1}{2}''$ x 4''—bottom ⎭
1 pc $\frac{1}{16}''$ x $\frac{3}{4}''$ x $2\frac{1}{8}''$—dashboard
2 pc $\frac{1}{16}''$ x $\frac{1}{4}''$ x $1\frac{3}{8}''$—dashboard holders
2 pc $\frac{1}{8}''$ x $\frac{1}{4}''$ x $3\frac{9}{16}''$—seat supports
2 pc $\frac{1}{4}''$ x 1'' x 2''—seat backs, A
2 pc $\frac{1}{4}''$ x $\frac{3}{4}''$ x 2''—seat, B
4 pc $\frac{1}{16}''$ x $\frac{1}{2}''$ x 1''—seat sides, C
2 pc $\frac{1}{4}''$ x 1'' x 5''—for runners
6 pc $\frac{1}{8}''$ dowel 1'' long
3 pc $\frac{1}{4}''$ x $\frac{1}{8}''$ x $2\frac{1}{2}''$—box supports or cross braces
1 pc $\frac{1}{4}''$ x $\frac{1}{4}''$ x $1\frac{7}{8}''$—crosspiece between runners
2 pc $\frac{1}{16}''$ x $\frac{1}{8}''$ x 5''—shafts
1 pc $\frac{1}{16}''$ x $\frac{1}{4}''$ x $2\frac{1}{4}''$—A ⎫ shaft crossbar
2 pc $\frac{1}{16}''$ x $\frac{1}{4}''$ x $2\frac{1}{2}''$—B ⎭
1 pc $\frac{1}{8}''$ x $\frac{1}{8}''$ x 2'' long—singletree

Construction:

1. Make the box by gluing the sides to the ends. Then glue the bottom board to the sides and ends. The bottom will extend about $\frac{3}{16}''$ on either side.

2. Glue the dashboard holders against the inside of the front end. Set the dashboard on the front end, and glue it to the two holders.

3. Glue a seat support to the inside of the box $\frac{1}{16}''$ down from the upper edge of each side.

4. Make the seats by gluing piece B to piece A. Be sure

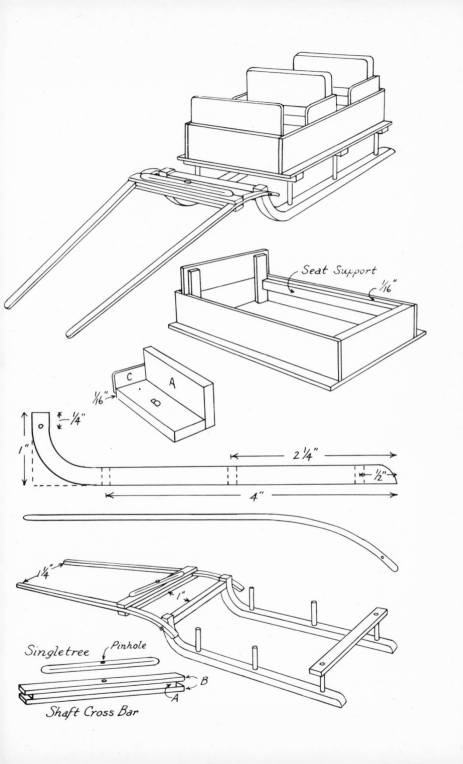

Seat Support

1/16"

C
A
B

1/16"

1/4"

1"

2 1/4"

1/2"

4"

1 1/4"

1"

Singletree

Pinhole

B

A

Shaft Cross Bar

that the seats fit in between the sides of the box. Glue on the sides $\frac{1}{16}''$ up from the underside of the seat board. When set in place, the sides will rest on the upper edges of the box. Glue the back seat in place against the back end of the box and the front seat about $\frac{5}{8}''$ in front of it.

5. Saw out the runners, using the diagram as a guide.

6. Drill three $\frac{1}{8}''$ holes in each runner as shown. Also drill the hole at the curved end with a no. 60 drill.

7. Drive a piece of dowel into each of the $\frac{1}{8}''$ holes in the runners.

8. Drill a $\frac{1}{8}''$ hole in each box support $\frac{1}{4}''$ in from each end. Attach the runners to the box supports.

9. Center the crosspiece between the curved ends of the runners and between the holes drilled in the runners. Glue in place.

10. Soak the shafts in water and bend to the shape shown. Drill a no. 60 hole in each shaft $\frac{1}{4}''$ from the curved end.

11. Make the shaft crossbar by gluing piece A in between the two B pieces, which will extend $\frac{1}{8}''$ beyond piece A at each end.

12. Drill a small hole for a pin or toothpick in the center of the singletree and the crossbar.

13. Attach the shafts to the runners with pieces of pins inserted through the holes in the shafts and into the crossbar between the runners.

14. Glue the shaft crossbar between the shafts and about $1''$ from the back or curved end of the shafts. A rubber band will hold the shafts in the desired position until the glue sets.

15. Shape the singletree and fasten it to the shaft crossbar with a toothpick or a piece cut from a pin.

A Plank Road

Roads in America were built of various materials, including crushed oyster shells and charcoal. Logs were laid side by side to form the corduroy roads. The first plank road from Syracuse, New York, to Oneida Lake was opened to travel in 1846. By the latter part of the nineteenth century, there were hundreds of miles of plank roads in the country. Such a road would last for several years, depending on the kind of wood used.

The first plank roads were usually toll roads and were built of planks three to four inches in thickness and of varying widths. The planks were laid side by side on sleepers, or rails, and every other plank extended about four inches. This permitted the wagon wheels to get back on the road if they ran off and also warned the driver that he was close to the edge of the road.

Even today, many decades after the plank roads have rotted away, some highways are still known as "The Plank Road."

A Plank Road

Materials:

    2 pc ¼″ x ⅜″ x 8″—sleepers (or rails)
    16 pc ⅛″ x ½″ x 3″—planks

Construction:

    1. Glue the planks to the sleepers so as to form irregular edges as shown below. The planks extend ⅛″. Space the sleepers 1½″ apart.

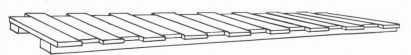

"Kissing Bridges"

The earliest bridges in America were logs laid across streams with other logs placed on them to form a "corduroy" bridge. As it became necessary to span wider streams and rivers, the truss-type bridge was constructed. The truss design was based on the triangle, which cannot be forced out of shape under pressure.

The first structures were only partially covered to protect the wood from the weather. In the early nineteenth century, the heyday of the covered bridge in America, the builders began to cover the entire bridge. Covered bridges soon began to dot the countryside as hundreds of them were built, many of which are still standing today. Others, ravaged by time, have been razed to make way for modern structures of stone, concrete, or steel.

Covered bridges provided shelter in time of storm and a cool place to rest the horse during the hot days of summer. They were also known as "kissing bridges" in those horse-and-buggy days, for obvious reasons. The majority of the bridges were built by private companies, and toll was collected from those who passed through.

Ingenious carpenters, architects, and craftsmen designed a variety of trusses to replace the simple king-post truss, which was adequate for short bridges but not suitable for longer spans. Among the trusses designed, some of which were patented, were the queen-post, multiple king-post, and lattice truss. The latter, invented by Ithiel Town, an architect in New Haven, Connecticut, consisted of diagonal planks crisscrossed to form a series of triangles. Town patented the design, which he called the "Town Lattice

Mode." This shrewd Yankee collected a dollar a foot for any bridge built according to his design. The Town lattice truss was widely used in many parts of the country.

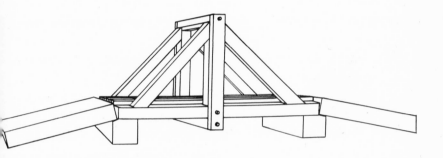

An Open King-Post Bridge

Materials:

2 pc ⅜″ x ⅜″ x 6½″—chords
2 pc ⅜″ x ⅜″ x 2¾″—king posts
2 pc ¼″ x ⅜″ x 3¾″—braces
1 pc ¼″ x ⅜″ x 3¾″—A ⎫
1 pc ⅛″ x ⅜″ x 3″—B ⎭ top cross brace
5 pc ⅜″ x ⅜″ x 3″—floor cross braces
8 pc ⅛″ x ⅜″ x 6½″—flooring
1 pc ⅜″ x ⅜″ x 3¾″—under cross brace
2 pc ⅛″ x ⅜″ x 3¾″—king post side pieces
2 pc ¾″ x ¾″ x 3¾″—abutments or piers
2 pc ½″ x 3¾″ x 4″—ramps

Construction:

1. Glue a king post to the center of each chord and a brace to the side of each king post. Cut the ends of the braces at 45-degree angles. See the diagram.

2. Fasten the two side assemblies together by gluing the braces between them, one brace at each end, one at the center, and the last two equally spaced between the king posts and the ends.

3. Make the top cross brace by fastening piece B to piece A ⅜″ in from one end of A.

4. Glue the top brace to the upper ends of the king posts.

5. Glue the floorboards to the cross braces.

6. Glue the under cross brace to the underside of the center brace and the chords.

7. Glue the side pieces to the king posts and ends of the top and under braces. Drill holes for round toothpick pegs (trunnels) as shown.

8. Make one corner of each abutment slightly slanted, and glue an abutment to each end of the bridge with the slanted corner out. The ramps may be glued to the abutments.

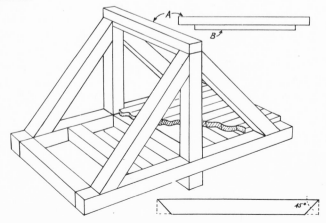

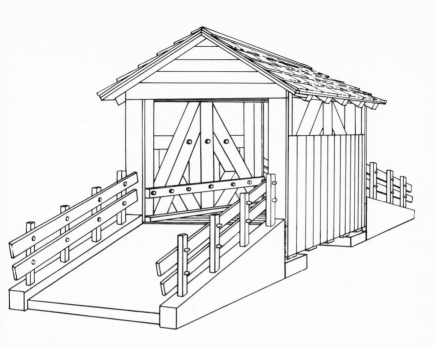

A King-Post Truss Covered Bridge

Materials:

    6 pc $\frac{3}{8}$" x $\frac{3}{8}$" x $2\frac{3}{4}$"—king posts and end posts

    4 pc $\frac{3}{8}$" x $\frac{3}{8}$" x $3\frac{7}{8}$"—long braces

    4 pc $\frac{3}{8}$" x $\frac{3}{8}$" x $1\frac{9}{16}$"—short braces

    2 pc $\frac{3}{8}$" x $\frac{3}{8}$" x $6\frac{5}{8}$"—lower chords

    2 pc $\frac{1}{4}$" x $\frac{3}{8}$" x $6\frac{5}{8}$"—upper chords

    3 pc $\frac{1}{4}$" x $\frac{3}{8}$" x $6\frac{5}{8}$"—floor supports

    2 pc $\frac{1}{8}$" x $\frac{1}{4}$" x $6\frac{5}{8}$"—y, inside strips

    4 pc $\frac{1}{16}$" x $\frac{3}{8}$" x $6\frac{5}{8}$"—x, outside strips

    5 pc $\frac{1}{4}$" x $\frac{3}{8}$" x $3\frac{3}{4}$"—A   ⎫
                                ⎬ lower cross braces

    10 pc $\frac{3}{8}$" x $\frac{3}{8}$" x $1\frac{1}{8}$"—B ⎭

    8 pc $\frac{1}{4}$" x $\frac{1}{4}$" x $3\frac{3}{4}$"—C   ⎫

    8 pc $\frac{1}{4}$" x $\frac{1}{4}$" x 3"—D   ⎬ upper cross braces

    2 pc $\frac{1}{8}$" x $\frac{1}{4}$" x 3"—E   ⎭

6 pc ⅛″ x ½″ x 6⅝″—floorboards (3″ long if crossways)

2 pc ⅛″ x ⅛″ x 6⅝″—floor strips

10 pc ⅛″ x ¼″ x 2¾″—rafters

8 pc ¹⁄₁₆″ x ¼″ x 2½″—rafter braces

¹⁄₁₆″ material ¼″ to ⅜″ wide—for siding

12 pc ¹⁄₁₆″ x ⅜″ x 7⅛″—roof boards

¹⁄₃₂″ wood (or ¹⁄₆₄″ if available)—for shingles

Construction:

1. Glue a king post to the center of each lower chord and an end post to each end of the chord.

2. Saw each end of the long braces at a 45-degree angle. Glue them in place between the king posts and end posts. Saw one end of the short braces at a 45-degree angle and set them against the long brace and on the lower chord.

3. Fasten the upper chords to the ends of the posts.

4. Glue a floor support to one side of each lower chord. This will be the inside of the bridge.

5. Fasten with toothpick pegs the inside strips y to the posts and braces ⅞″ up from the lower chords.

6. Glue one of the outside strips x to the posts and braces 1⅝″ up from the lower chord and another one to the outer side of the chord. The siding boards will be glued to these strips, leaving an opening at the top of the bridge.

7. Prepare five lower cross braces, to tie the sides together, by gluing two 1⅛″ B pieces to each A piece ⅝″ from the ends of A. This will leave a ¼″ wide opening at the center for the middle floor support.

8. Make the upper cross braces by gluing a D piece to each C piece ⅜″ in from one end of the C piece. On two of the cross braces, glue an E piece to one side of each of

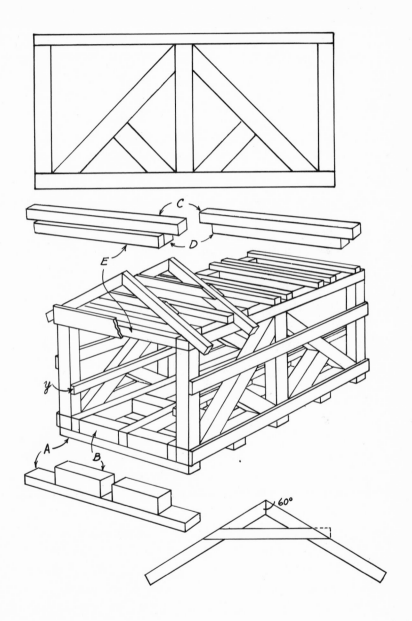

C

D

E

y

A

B

60°

two of the D pieces. These two braces will be used at either end of the bridge.

9. Tie the sides together by gluing a lower cross brace in position at each end of the bridge. Also set in place the upper end braces with the E piece toward the outside of the ends of the bridge. Make certain that the outer edges of all braces are even with the ends of the upper and lower chords. Rubber bands will hold the sides firmly together until the glue has set.

10. Install the three remaining lower cross braces, one at the center under the king posts and the others spaced evenly between the center brace and end braces. Install the center floor support.

11. Put in the upper cross braces, two at the center and the others spaced evenly between the center and end braces. The three pairs of braces should be spaced $\frac{1}{8}''$ apart to allow the rafters to fit between them. It is a good idea to glue one brace in place, and when set, add the second brace $\frac{1}{8}''$ away. Use a rafter or piece of $\frac{1}{8}''$ stock as a measure.

12. Glue the floorboards to the floor supports. Fasten the $\frac{1}{8}''$ x $\frac{1}{8}''$ x $6\frac{5}{8}''$ floor strips to the floor and against the posts and braces on either side.

13. Cut the rafters, using the diagram as a guide. Glue the slanted ends together, and when set, glue a cross brace to each side of three pairs of rafters about $\frac{1}{2}''$ down from the peak. Glue only one brace to the other two pairs of rafters. These will be the end rafters, and when put in position, the crosspiece should be to the inside. Trim off any corners of the braces that extend above the rafters.

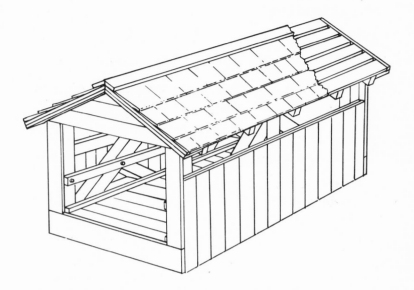

14. Glue a piece of the siding material $\frac{1}{16}''$ x $\frac{1}{2}''$ x $4''$ to each end of the bridge so that the lower edge of the piece is even with the lower edge of the end cross brace and the ends of the upper chords. It will extend $\frac{1}{8}''$ at each end. This will make a place for the end pair of rafters to fit into.

15. Glue the end rafters (the ones with one brace) in place. Be sure that the peak of the rafters is in the exact center of the bridge and the brace is to the inside. Install the other rafters in between the cross braces, again making sure that the peaks are in a straight line.

16. Cover the sides of the bridge first with pieces of siding $2\frac{1}{2}''$ long glued to the two outside strips. Cover the lower end cross braces and ends of the chords with a piece $\frac{3}{4}''$ wide by $4''$ long (or two pieces $\frac{3}{8}''$ wide). Cover the

end posts with pieces ½″ x 2⅝″ long. Complete the gable end, allowing the siding to extend a little beyond the upper surface of the end rafters. Cut off these ends before applying the roof boards.

17. Glue the roof boards to the rafters leaving a little space between the boards.

18. Box in the ends of the roof boards and shingle the roof. See the Introduction (pages 15–17).

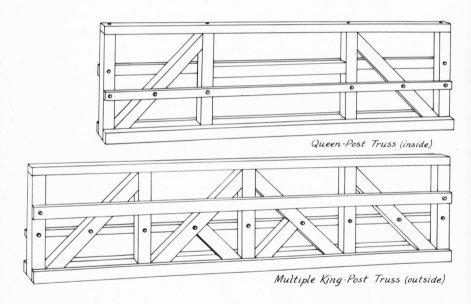

Queen-Post Truss (inside)

Multiple King-Post Truss (outside)

A King-Post Truss Covered Bridge Approach

Materials:

4 pc ⅜″ x 1½″ x 4″—side pieces
2 pc ⅜″ x ⅞″ x 3¼″—A, cross brace
2 pc ⅜″ x ¾″ x 4″—bridge piers
2 pc ¼″ x 3¼″ x 4″—road boards
16 pc ⅛″ x ⅛″ x 1½″—fence posts
8 pc ¹⁄₁₆″ x ¼″ x 4″—fence boards

Construction:

1. Make the side pieces (see the diagram) and drill four ⅛″ holes about ⅜″ in depth in each for the fence posts. Start the first hole ¼″ from the wider end, and space the other three holes 1⅛″ apart and in a straight line.

2. Glue the side sections to the ends of the cross brace.

3. Glue a pier to the front edge of the cross brace and ends of the sides.

4. Set the "road" board in between the sides and glue it to the sides and the crosspiece. The upper ends of this board should be rounded off with a file and sandpaper. Rubber bands will hold the approach assembly together until the glue sets.

5. Round off one end of the posts and drive them into the holes drilled in the side pieces, allowing each post to extend above the side piece 1¼″. Be sure that a flat side of the post faces to the inside. Glue the boards to the inside of the posts. When glue has set, the posts and boards can be drilled with a small drill and flat toothpick pegs put through the boards and into the posts.

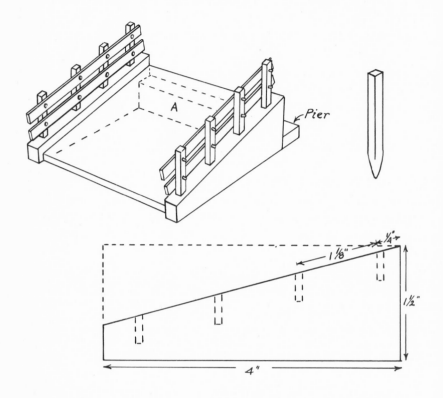

A Lattice Truss Covered Bridge

Materials:

4 pc ¼″ x ¾″ x 14″—lower chords
4 pc ¼″ x ½″ x 14″—upper chords
8 pc ¼″ x ½″ x 2¾″—upright posts
48 pc ⅛″ x ⅜″ x 5″ ⎫
8 pc ⅛″ x ⅜″ x 3″ ⎬ lattice planks
2 pc ¼″ x ¼″ x 13″—outside strips to hold siding

4 pc ¼″ x ¾″ x 4½″—A ⎫
4 pc ⅜″ x ¾″ x 3″—B ⎬ end cross braces
2 pc ⅛″ x ⅜″ x 3″—C ⎭

3 pc ¼″ x ¾″ x 3½″—x ⎫ lower cross braces
3 pc ⅜″ x ¾″ x 3″—y ⎭

1 pc ⅜″ x ⅜″ x 14″ ⎫ floor support
4 pc ⅜″ x¾″ x 1⁵⁄₁₆″—spacers ⎭

16 pc ⅛″ x ¾″ x 3½″ ⎫ floorboards
2 pc ⅛″ x ½″ x 3″ ⎭

2 pc ¼″ x ¼″ x 13″—inside floor strips

14 pc ¼″ x ¼″ x 4½″—A ⎫ upper cross braces and rafter
14 pc ¼″ x ¼″ x 3″—B ⎭ holders

18 pc ⅛″ x ¼″ x 3¼″ ⎫ rafters and cross braces
16 pc ¹⁄₁₆″ x ¼″ x 3″ ⎭

4 pc ¹⁄₁₆″ x ½″ x 4¼″—siding for posts

74–75 pc ¹⁄₁₆″ x ⅜″ x 2¹³⁄₁₆″—siding

¹⁄₁₆″ x ⅜″ x length required—siding material for ends

20 pc ¹⁄₁₆″ x ¼″ x 14⅜″—roof boards

¹⁄₃₂″ wood (or ¹⁄₆₄″ if available)—for shingles

Round toothpicks—for trunnels

Construction:

1. Make four frames by gluing one upper chord and one lower chord together with a post at each end.

2. Draw lines on two of the frames for the two sides of the bridge as shown. Draw line AB. Then using a piece of wood ⅞″ wide as a straight edge and spacer, draw lines CD, EF, GH, etc. Also draw line XY. Draw dotted line MN, which will later serve as a guide when putting on the second row of planks.

3. Glue the first row of planks to the frame starting on

the left side of line XY. Glue each plank in place on the left side of lines AB, CD, EF, etc. Each plank will extend above the upper chord about ⅛″.

4. Using line MN as a guide, draw lines PQ, RS, TU, etc., on the first row of planks, again using the ⅞″ piece as before.

5. Glue the second row of planks to the first row, making sure that they extend beyond the chords the same distance as the first row. Except for two planks at either end, each plank will cross five other planks. Cut off the ends of any planks that extend beyond the posts at the ends of the side sections. It may be necessary to glue short filler pieces to the posts under the last one or two planks.

6. Drill two no. 45 holes in the planks where they cross each other (except at either end) and insert the trunnels into these holes. There will be six in each plank. The ends of the lower row of trunnels on the inside of the bridge should be flush with the surface of the planks. Otherwise, they will interfere with a piece that will be put on the

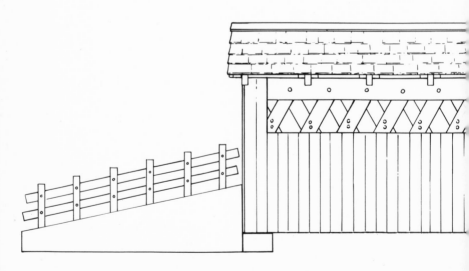

floor, against the planks. Let the ends of other trunnels extend slightly beyond surface of planks.

7. Construct the other side of the bridge the same way. The first row of planks will run in the opposite direction from the first row on the side just completed.

8. Glue one of the other frames to each of the lattice assemblies, making certain that the two frames, when put together, are even at the ends and top.

9. Drill holes through the upper and lower chords where the planks cross. Drive trunnels through these holes. The ends of the trunnels in the lower outside chords must be even with the surface of the chords so they will not interfere with the siding.

10. Make four end cross braces, two for the top and two for the bottom of the bridge, by gluing piece B to piece A. Then glue a C piece to one side of each of two of the B pieces.

11. Tie the two sides together by first gluing the lower end braces in position, making sure that the front edge of

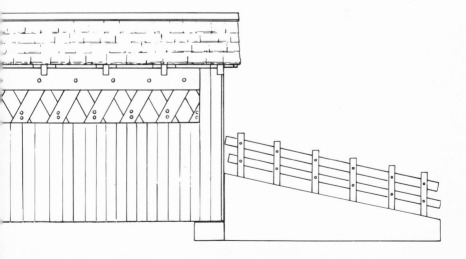

the brace is even with the ends of the lower chords. It will be necessary to cut off the protruding ends of the last few planks to make room for the cross braces. When the glue has set, install the top braces in the same way with the C pieces to the front of the bridge and flush with the ends of the upper chords.

12. Make the three other braces by gluing piece y to piece x. Fasten one of these to the center of the underside of the bridge between the two inside chords and the others midway between the center brace and the end braces.

13. Glue a spacer to the upper side of each lower end cross brace, then the floor support, and then another spacer.

14. Glue the floorboards to the inside chords and the center support. Use the two shorter boards at the ends of the bridge. Glue the two inside strips to the floor and against the lattice.

15. Make the upper braces by gluing piece B to piece A $\frac{3}{4}''$ in from one end of A. Glue these braces in pairs, $\frac{1}{8}''$ apart, to the upper chords. Use a piece of $\frac{1}{8}''$ material as a spacer so the rafters will fit in between the cross braces. Begin with the center pair and space the other pairs equally between the center and the end braces or about $1\frac{5}{8}''$ apart. It will be necessary to cut off the ends of planks that protrude above the chords and are in the way of the braces and rafters. It is also best to glue one brace in place and, when set, add the other one $\frac{1}{8}''$ from it.

16. Make the rafters using the drawing as a guide to cut the slanted end at a 60-degree angle. Glue them together at the peak. Fasten two cross braces one on either side, about $\frac{5}{8}''$ down from the peak, to seven pairs of rafters. Put only one cross brace on the two remaining pairs.

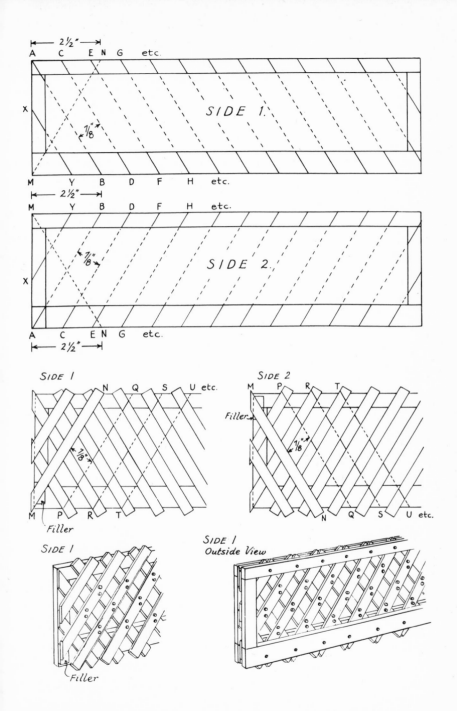

2½"
A   C   E N G etc.

X

⅛"

SIDE 1.

M   Y   B   D   F   H   etc.
2½"

M   Y   B   D   F   H   etc.
2½"

X

⅛"

SIDE 2.

A   C   E N G etc.
2½"

SIDE 1
N   Q   S   U etc.
⅛"
M   P   R   T
Filler

SIDE 2
M   P   R   T
Filler
⅛"
N   Q   S   U etc.

SIDE 1
Filler

SIDE 1
Outside View

17. Glue a piece of siding ½″ wide and 4⅝″ long to the C pieces on the end cross braces and to the ends of the upper chords. These pieces will extend 1/16″ beyond the outside chord on each side of the bridge. This piece of siding will make a place for the end rafters to fit into, thus making it easier to install.

18. Glue a pair of rafters with one cross brace at each end of the bridge, with the cross brace to the inside. Make sure that the peaks are exactly in the center of the bridge. Set and glue the other rafters in place, being certain that all peaks are in a straight line.

19. The siding and shape of the entrance of the old bridges varied according to the men who were building them. Some bridges were sided all the way to the roof, while others were sided only part way up. This model is of the latter type, showing the lattice truss. Entrances also varied, as shown in the diagrams. If entrance A is selected, it will be necessary to glue two ¼″ x ¼″ x 1″ pieces cut at 45-degree angles at each end, as shown.

20. Glue an outside strip to each side 1½″ up from the lower chord, to which the siding will be fastened.

21. Cover the sides of the end posts with the 4¼″ strips of siding.

22. Apply the shorter boards to the sides, making any necessary adjustments due to possible varying widths of materials.

23. If bridge entrance A is being made, first cover the braces and the upper ends of the posts with pieces of horizontal siding. Cut a 45-degree angle on the end of a piece of siding and then cut to the length needed.

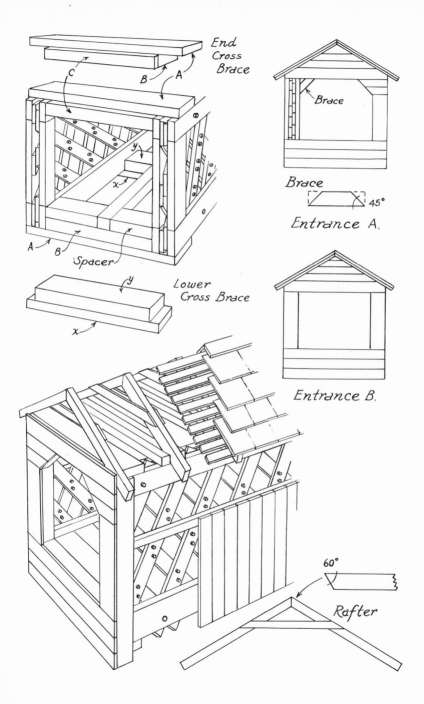

End
Cross
Brace

C

B

A

y

x

A

B

Spacer

Lower
Cross Brace

y

x

Brace

Brace
45°

Entrance A.

Entrance B.

60°

Rafter

24. Next cover the lower end of the bridge with pieces 4⅝" long. These end boards will extend over the edges of the sideboards on the posts. Glue a vertical strip $^{13}/_{16}$" wide and about 2⅛" long to the posts.

25. Finish siding the gable end by letting each piece extend a little way beyond the upper edge of the end rafters. Cut these ends off even with the edge of the rafters.

26. Put on the roof boards, leaving a little space between them and box in the ends. See the Introduction (pages 15–16).

27. Shingle the roof. See the Introduction (pages 16–17).

Lattice Bridge Approaches

Materials:

    4 pc ½" x 2" x 6"—sides
    2 pc ½" x 1¼" x 3¾"—cross braces
    2 pc ½" x ¾" x 4¾"—piers
    2 pc ¼" x 3¾" x 6"—roadway
    24 pc $^{3}/_{16}$" x $^{3}/_{16}$" x 1½"—fence posts
    8 pc $^{1}/_{16}$" x ¼" x 6"—fence boards

Construction:

1. Make the sides of the approaches as shown in the diagram. If a fence is built, drill six $^{3}/_{16}$" holes about ⅜" in depth in a straight line on the slanted edge of each side piece. Start the first hole ½" from one end and space the holes 1" apart.

2. Glue the side sections to the ends of the cross brace, which goes between the wider ends. Keep the lower edge

of the brace even with the lower edges of the sides. See the diagram.

3. Glue the pier to the front edge of the brace and the ends of the sides.

4. Set the "road" board in between the sides, and glue it to the sides and brace. A strong rubber band will hold the assembly together until the glue hardens. Refer to the diagram of the King-Post Truss Covered Bridge Approach on page 110.

5. Round off one end of the posts. Drive them into the holes drilled in the side pieces, allowing each post to extend above the side piece 1¼". Be sure that a flat side of the post faces to the inside. Glue the boards to the inside of the posts about ¼" apart. When the glue has set, the posts and boards can be drilled and flat toothpick pegs put through the boards and into the posts.

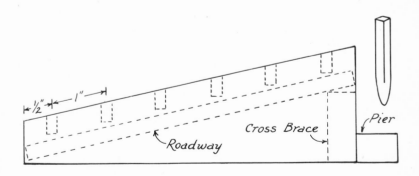

Cross Brace   Pier

Roadway

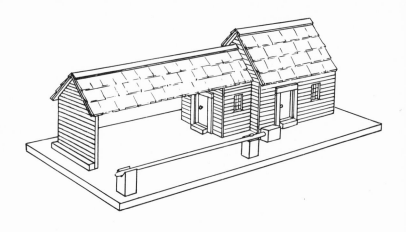

A Tollhouse and Pike

Today many of our highways are called turnpikes. The word turnpike comes from the turnstile used on early toll roads and covered bridges. A pike or bar was turned or raised to allow travelers access to the road or bridge. Turnpikes were usually built by companies who charged toll to those who used them. Turnpike building was so popular that many companies were incorporated and sold shares of stock to investors.

A Tollhouse and Pike

Materials for main building:

    2 pc ⅛″ x 3″ x 2¼″—ends
    2 pc ¹⁄₁₆″ x 1¾″ x 3¼″—sides
    1 pc ¼″ x 2¼″ x 3″—floor

2 pc ⅛″ x ⅝″ x 1″—doors
2 pc ¹⁄₁₆″ x ⅛″ x ⅝″—lower supports
2 pc ⅛″ x ⅛″ x ⅝″—upper supports
2 pc ¹⁄₁₆″ x ⅛″ x 1″—sides ⎤ frame,
⎟ inside
1 pc ¹⁄₁₆″ x ⅛″ x ¾″—top ⎦ door
1 pc ¹⁄₁₆″ x ⅛″ x ½″—inside sill
2 pc ¹⁄₁₆″ x ⅛″ x 1¼″—sides ⎤ frame,
⎟ outside
1 pc ¹⁄₁₆″ x ⅛″ x ¾″—top ⎦ door   ⎬ door assemblies
1 pc ⅛″ x ⁵⁄₁₆″ x ½″—outside sill
1 pc ⅛″ x ⅛″ x ½″—step
2 small nails—knobs
2 pins or paper clips—hinges
10 pc ¹⁄₁₆″ x ¼″ x 3½″—roof boards
¹⁄₆₄″ or ¹⁄₃₂″ wood—for shingles

Materials for toll collector's booth and shelter:

3 pc ⅛″ x 2½″ x 1¾″—ends, roof support
2 pc ¹⁄₁₆″ x 1½″ x 1¼″—sides
1 pc ¼″ x 1¾″ x 1⅛″—floor
1 pc ¼″ x ¼″ x 1¾″—A
2 pc ⅛″ x ¼″ x 1¼″—B
1 pc ⅛″ x ⅝″ x 1″—door
1 pc ¹⁄₁₆″ x ⅛″ x ⅝″—lower support
1 pc ⅛″ x ⅛″ x ⅝″—upper support
1 pc ⅛″ x ⁵⁄₁₆″ x ½″—sill
1 pc ⅛″ x ⅛″ x ½″—step   ⎬ door assembly
1 small nail—knob
2 pc ¹⁄₁₆″ x ⅛″ x 1¼″—sides ⎤ frame
1 pc ¹⁄₁₆″ x ⅛″ x ¾″—top ⎦
2 pins or paper clips—hinges

8 pc $\frac{1}{16}$″ x $\frac{1}{4}$″ x $5\frac{1}{2}$″—roof boards

$\frac{1}{64}$″ or $\frac{1}{32}$″ wood—for shingles

2 pc $\frac{1}{2}$″ x $\frac{1}{2}$″ x $\frac{3}{4}$″—posts

1 pc $\frac{1}{2}$″ x $\frac{1}{2}$″ x $\frac{5}{8}$″—weight

1 pc $\frac{1}{8}$″ dowel $5\frac{1}{2}$″ long   pike assembly

1 small nail or pin

1 pc $\frac{1}{4}$″ x $4\frac{1}{2}$″ x 10″—mounting board

Construction of main building:

1. Using the diagram as a guide, saw out the ends. Make a $\frac{1}{2}$″ by $1\frac{1}{4}$″ opening in the center of one end for the doorway.

2. Cut the openings for the door and windows in the side pieces. See the diagram for the location of the openings.

3. With an awl or sharp nail, make lines about $\frac{1}{8}$″ apart to represent siding.

4. Glue the ends to the floor and the sides to the floor and the ends.

5. Hang the doors and install the windows. See the Introduction (pages 12–14).

6. Frame the doors and glue the outside sill to the edge of the floor. Glue the inside sill in place.

Construction of toll collector's booth and shelter:

1. Saw out three end sections, using the diagram as a guide.

2. Make the openings for the windows in the side pieces.

3. Draw lines as before to represent siding.

4. Glue the A piece to the outside of one end section, even with the lower edge of the end.

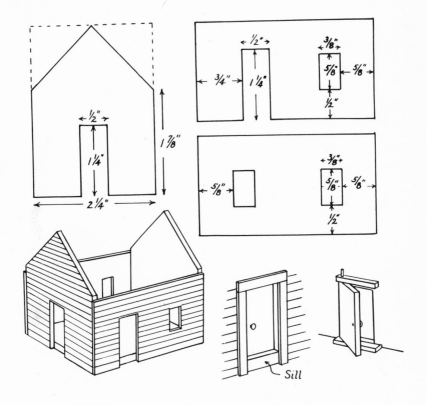

5. Cut a piece 1″ long from the peak end of another section for roof support. See the diagram.

6. Make a ½″ by 1¼″ opening for the doorway in the remaining end piece.

7. Glue the end with the doorway to the end of the floor. Center and glue the other end of the tollbooth floor to the end of the building.

8. Center and glue the roof support to the doorway end

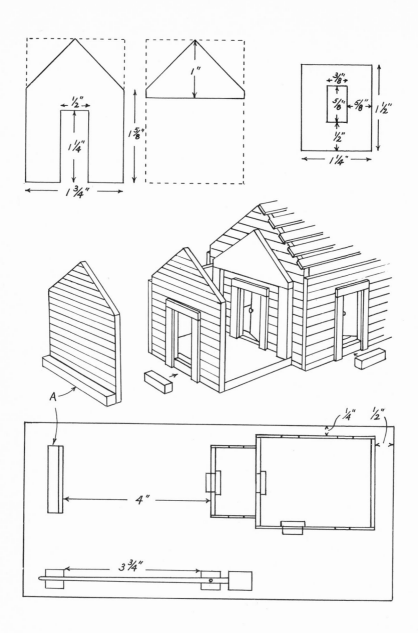

of the main building. It should be 1½″ from the lower edge of the end and ½″ down from the peak, in line with it.

9. Glue the two B pieces to the end of the building ¼″ from each side edge and against the lower end of the roof support.

10. Glue the sides of the tollbooth to the end, floor, and B pieces.

11. Hang the door and install the windows. See the Introduction (pages 12–14).

12. Frame the door and glue the sill to the edge of floor.

13. Glue the assembled house and tollbooth ½″ in from one end and ¼″ from one edge of the mounting board. Glue steps in front of doorsills.

14. Glue the end of the shelter to the mounting board 4″ from the end of the booth and in line with it.

15. Put the roof boards on the two sections of the tollhouse. Box in the ends and shingle the roofs. See the Introduction (pages 15–17).

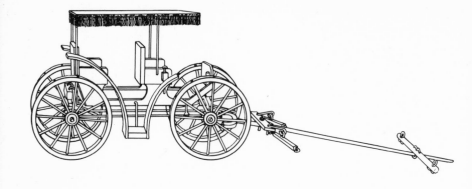

A Fringed-Top Surrey

The surrey was a light four-wheeled pleasure carriage with two seats, and most had a rigid fringed top. Drawn by one or two horses, it was a popular means of transportation in the United States between 1880 and 1910. This graceful vehicle was somewhat like an English carriage built in Surrey, England.

Soon after the beginning of the twentieth century, the surrey "with the fringe on top" was gradually replaced by the "horseless carriage."

A Fringed-Top Surrey

Materials:

2 pc $\frac{1}{16}''$ x $\frac{3}{4}''$ x $4\frac{1}{2}''$—for sides
1 pc $\frac{3}{16}''$ x $1\frac{1}{2}''$ x $3\frac{3}{4}''$—A $\Big\}$ floor
1 pc $\frac{3}{16}''$ x $1\frac{1}{2}''$ x $\frac{3}{4}''$—B
2 pc $\frac{1}{8}''$ x $\frac{3}{4}''$ x $1\frac{1}{2}''$—body cross braces
1 pc $\frac{1}{32}''$ x $1''$ x $1\frac{5}{8}''$—dashboard
1 pc $\frac{1}{32}''$ x $\frac{3}{4}''$ x $1\frac{5}{8}''$—back end
1 pc $\frac{1}{8}''$ x $\frac{1}{8}''$ x $1\frac{1}{2}''$—body hanger holder

1 pc ⅛″ dowel ½″ long—whip socket

2 pc ⅛″ x 1″ x 1¾″—bottom ⎤

2 pc ⅛″ x 1⅜″ x 2″—backs ⎟

4 pc ⅛″ x ⅝″ x 1″—sides ⎬ seats

2 pc ⅛″ x 1″ x 1¾″—cushions ⎦

1 pc ⅛″ x 2¼″ x 4½″—roof ⎤

2 pc ⅛″ x ¼″ x 4⅜″—frame, sides ⎟

2 pc ⅛″ x ¼″ x 1⅞″—frame, ends ⎬ top

1 pc ¾″ black ribbon about 15″ long—fringe ⎟

4 pc wire 2¼″ long—roof supports ⎦

2 pc ³⁄₁₆″ x ⅜″ x 3″—axletrees

1 pc ³⁄₁₆″ x ¼″ x 2¼″—rear bolster

1 pc ¼″ x ¼″ x 1½″—front bolster

1 pc ³⁄₁₆″ x ³⁄₁₆″ x 1½″—bed piece

2 pc ³⁄₁₆″ x ½″ x 2¼″—for springs

1 pc ¹⁄₁₆″ x ¾″ x ¾″—for fifth wheel

2 pc ¹⁄₁₆″ dowel 5″ long—tie rods

2 pc ¹⁄₃₂″ x ⅜″ x 3½″—rear mudguards

2 pc ¹⁄₃₂″ x ⅜″ x 2″—front mudguards

2 pc ⅛″ x ½″ x ¾″—steps

2 pc ³⁄₁₆″ x ³⁄₁₆″ x ¼″ ⎤
                        ⎬ lamps
2 pins ⎦

2 wheels 3″ diameter—rear

2 wheels 2⅞″ diameter—front

1 pc ¼″ x 1″ x 2¾″—for holder ⎤
                               ⎬ tongue assembly
1 pc ⅛″ dowel 7″ long—pole ⎦

1 pc ⅛″ x ¼″ x 2½″—A ⎤
                      ⎬ singletree (whippletree)
2 pc ⅛″ x ⅛″ x 1½″—B ⎦

1 pc ³⁄₁₆″ dowel 2½″ long ⎤
                          ⎬ neck yoke
3 pc fine wire ⎦

A few paper clips

Construction:

1. Draw the outline for the sides on the wood according to the diagram and saw out. A five-cent piece can be used to draw the curves. Glue the sides to the floor pieces, and glue the cross braces in between the sides, even with the upper edge of the sides. The seats will rest on these braces. Glue on the back end piece. Drill a hole at y, $1\frac{7}{8}''$ from the back end, for the mudguard hangers, and another hole at x, $3\frac{1}{2}''$ from the same end, for the steps. The size of the holes, as in later instances, will depend on the size of wire or paper clips being used.

2. Prepare the parts for the seats. Drill a hole for the front roof supports in two side pieces $\frac{1}{2}''$ from the back edge and $\frac{3}{8}''$ up from the lower edge. Also drill holes for the rear roof supports in each end of one seat back $\frac{3}{8}''$ up from the lower edge. This piece will be for the rear seat. Assemble the seats by gluing the sides to the bottom and then adding the backs. Round off all of the corners on one side of each cushion.

3. Shape the two body hangers from paper clips as shown. Drill two holes in the underside of the floor $1''$ from the rear end, $1''$ apart, and $\frac{1}{4}''$ from the side edges of floor. Insert the ends of the hangers into the holes, and glue the holder over them $\frac{1}{8}''$ in from the end of the body. The grooves made in the holder will be over the hangers and will keep them in place.

4. Using the drawings as guides, make the axletrees, springs, bolsters, bed piece, and fifth wheel. Drill holes in the end of each axletree $\frac{1}{8}''$ up from the lower edge for the pins or small nails that will be used as axles.

5. Glue the fifth wheel to the center of the front axletree.

Make two $\frac{1}{16}''$ or no. 45 holes in the bed piece 1″ apart for the tie rods. Glue one edge of a spring to the bed piece. Drill a hole for the king bolt (nail, wire, or pin) through the center of the bed piece and one side of the spring. Make the same size hole through the fifth wheel and center of the axletree. Also drill holes in the front axletree at a and b for staples made from small paper clips, to which the tongue or pole will be attached to the surrey.

6. In order to make the front bolster, it will be necessary

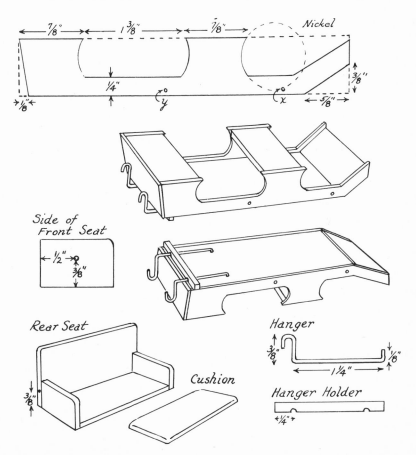

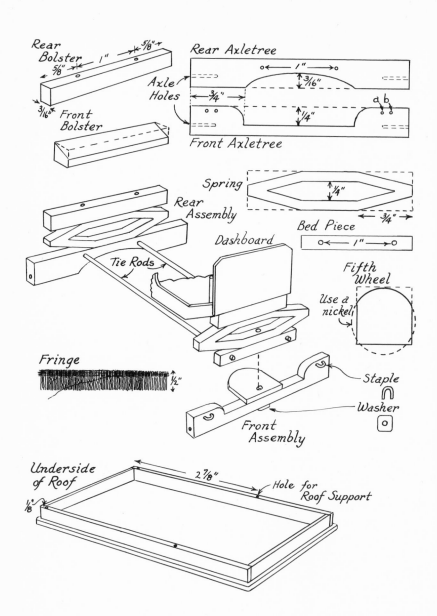

Rear Bolster
1"
5/8"
5/8"
3/16"
Front Bolster

Rear Axletree
Axle Holes
1"
3/16"
3/4"
Front Axletree
1/4"
a b

Spring
1/4"
3/4"

Rear Assembly

Dashboard

Bed Piece
1"

Fifth Wheel
Use a nickel

Tie Rods

Fringe
1/2"

Staple
Washer

Front Assembly

Underside of Roof
1/8"
2 7/8"
Hole for Roof Support

to file off one edge to make the same slant as the floorboard. When this edge is fastened to the front end of the floor, the lower side will make a flat surface for the spring to be glued to.

7. Drill holes in the rear bolster 1″ apart for the body hangers and in the rear axletree 1″ apart for the tie rods. Glue the spring to the axletree and the bolster to the spring.

8. File off the front end of the floorboard so that it is even with the front ends of the sides, and glue the dashboard to the front end.

9. Glue the front bolster to the underside of the floor even with the front end of the floor.

10. Glue the front spring and bed piece assembly to the bolster.

11. Glue the seats in place, allowing them to overhang about ⅛″ in front and back and ³⁄₁₆″ at each side.

12. Round off the corners of the roof. Glue the longer frame pieces to the roof ¹⁄₁₆″ in from the side edges and ends. Glue the other pieces between them ¹⁄₁₆″ from the ends of the roof. Drill holes for the wire roof supports ⅛″ in from one end of each side frame piece and also 2⅞″ from the same end.

13. Make the fringe by pulling threads or unraveling until it is about ½″ long. Glue the unraveled edge to the frame.

14. Insert the tie rods into the holes in the rear axletree and on through the holes in the bed piece. At the same time, put the curved ends of the body hangers into the holes in the rear bolster.

15. Insert a wire or piece of nail about ⅝″ in length up

through the front axletree, fifth wheel, bed piece, and lower part of the spring. Small wooden washers may be made and glued to the axletree and spring to make sure the "bolt" doesn't come out.

16. Insert the straight ends of the roof supports into the holes in the roof frame and then attach them to the seats.

17. Fasten the whip socket to the inside of the dashboard and against the right side of the surrey.

18. Shape the mudguards by soaking them and then fastening around a disk about 3½" in diameter. Hold with rubber bands until dry. Make a hole in the center of one side edge of each step for the hangers. Glue a front and a rear mudguard to opposite ends of the steps. Attach them to the sides with the hangers. For the front steps flatten the end of a piece of wire and bend as shown in the drawing.

19. Before sawing out the tongue holder, drill holes in each end for wire hooks and a ⅛" hole through the center for the pole.

20. Drill a hole for a pin 1" from one end of the pole. Taper the other end with sandpaper.

21. Insert the pole into the hole made for it in the holder and put short hooks, cut from paper clips, into the end holes.

22. To make the whippletree, drill a hole for a wire hook ¼" in from each end of the A piece and a hole in the center for the bolt. Drill two holes ⅛" apart in the center of the B pieces and a hole in the center of each end. Insert wire staples, cut from paper clips, into the center holes and wire hooks into the end holes. Fasten the B pieces to the A piece with wire hooks. Attach the whippletree to the tongue with a pin or small nail used as a bolt.

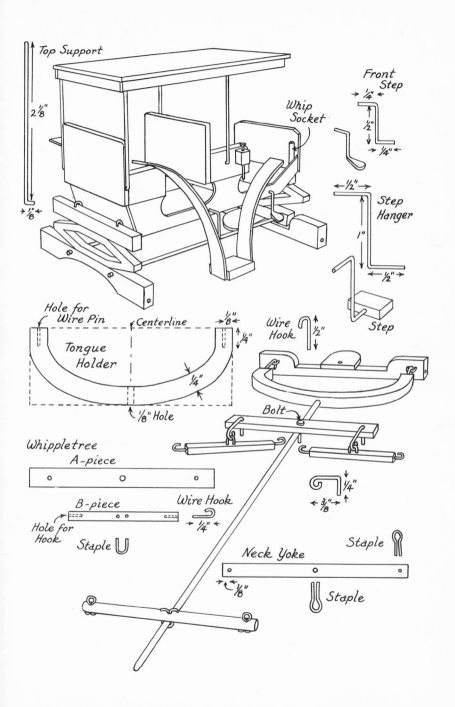

Top Support

2⅛"

⅛"

Front Step
¼"
½"
¼"

Whip Socket

Step Hanger
½"
1"
½"

Step

Hole for Wire Pin

Centerline

⅛"

¼"

Tongue Holder

¼"

⅛" Hole

Wire Hook
½"

Bolt

Whippletree
A-piece

¼"
3/8"

B-piece

Wire Hook

Hole for Hook

Staple ∪

¼"

Neck Yoke

⅛"

Staple

Staple

23. Make the neck yoke by drilling a hole ⅛″ in from each end and one in the center of the dowel. Make the loops from fine wire bent around a nail. Taper the neck yoke at the ends.

24. Make the lamps by drilling a hole in the center of each wooden piece and inserting a pin. Glue the lamps to the sides of the front seat and in front of the top support.

25. Paint or stain the body, roof, and running gear black.

26. Mount the wheels. See the Introduction (pages 10–12).

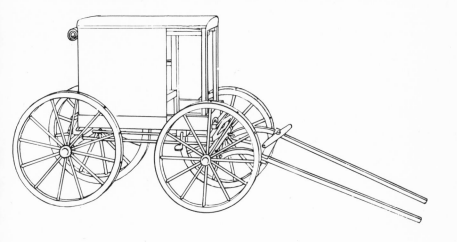

An Amish Family Buggy

In the early eighteenth century, religious groups, perse-
cuted in Europe because of their beliefs, settled in the
rolling hills and valleys of Pennsylvania, where William
Penn had promised religious freedom for all.

In their search for fertile lands to farm many of these
immigrants settled in Lancaster, Chester, and Berks coun-
ties in southeastern Pennsylvania, while others went farther
west to Ohio and Indiana.

The members of the group called the Amish are in-
dustrious farmers who do not believe in using tractors to
work their land but use horse-drawn equipment instead.
Neither do they believe in using automobiles for transportation, and the horse and Amish buggy are common sights
on the highways and in the villages of southeastern Pennsylvania.

An Amish Family Buggy

Materials for body:

2 pc ⅛″ x ½″ x 2⅜″—ends   ⎫
7 pc ¹⁄₁₆″ x ½″ x 4⅛″—sides and floor ⎬ box
8 pc ⅛″ x ⅛″ x 3″—studs
4 pc ⅛″ x ⅛″ x 1″—rear studs
6 pc ⅛″ x ⅛″ x 1⅛″—spacers
2 pc ⅛″ x ⅛″ x 2⅛″—box cross braces
2 pc ⅛″ x ¾″ x 2⅝″—seat supports
4 pc ⅛″ x ⅛″ x 2⅛″—roof cross braces
5 pc ⅛″ x ⅜″ x 2⅜″—roof supports
2 pc ¹⁄₁₆″ x ⅛″ x 3⅞″—inside lengthwise braces
1 pc ⅛″ x 1½″ x 2½″—back of body
2 pc ⅛″ x ½″ x 1⅛″—A ⎫
2 pc ¹⁄₁₆″ x ½″ x 1⅜″—B ⎬ seat sides
2 pc ¹⁄₁₆″ x ⅛″ x 2⅝″—outside body braces
2 pc ³⁄₁₆″ x ⅞″ x 2⅛″—seat
2 pc ³⁄₁₆″ x 1¼″ x 2⅛″—seat backs
2 pc ⅛″ x ⅛″ x ¾″— front seat guides
18 pc ¹⁄₁₆″ x ⅛″ x 4″—roof slats or ribbing
2 pc ⅛″ x ⅛″ x 4⅛″—body hanger supports
4 paper clips—for body hangers
2 pc ⅛″ x ¼″ x ¼″ ⎫
2 pins or pc of wire ⎬ steps
1 pc ¹⁄₁₆″ x ⅛″ x 4¼″—rod ⎫
2 pc ⅛″ x ³⁄₁₆″ x ½″—shoes ⎬ brake

Construction:

1. Make the box by gluing the sides to the ends and then adding the floorboards.

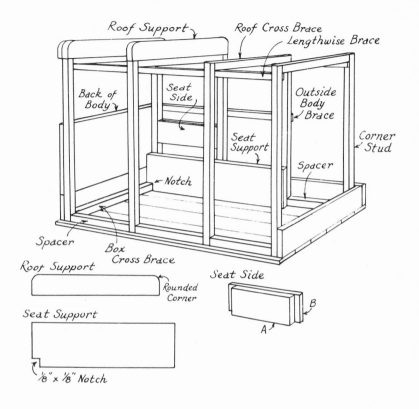

Roof Support   Roof Cross Brace
                      Lengthwise Brace

Back of   Seat
Body   Side   Outside
                                          Body
                 Seat   Brace
                 Support
                                                   Corner
                              Spacer   Stud

Notch

Spacer
          Box
Cross Brace

Roof Support   Seat Side

                    Rounded
                    Corner

Seat Support   B

                                          A

⅛″ x ⅛″ Notch

2. Glue the four corner studs to the floor and against the sides and ends of the box. Set the 2 ⅛″ braces against the ends of the box between the studs.

3. Glue a 1⅛″ spacer to the floor and against the side, then a stud, another spacer and so on.

4. Cut an ⅛″ x ⅛″ notch in one end of each seat support. Glue the supports to the studs, floor, and against the back end with the notch over the cross brace.

5. Round off the upper corners of the roof supports. To insure that they will all be alike, put all five in the vise and round off with sandpaper at the same time.

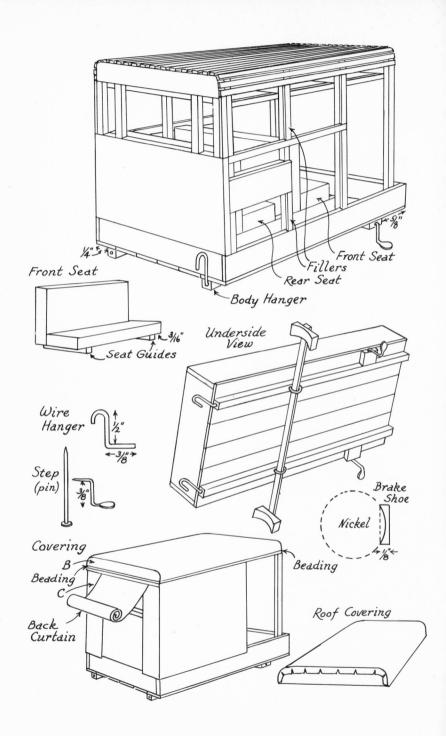

Front Seat

Rear Seat

Fillers

Front Seat

$\frac{5}{8}''$

$\frac{1}{4}''$

Body Hanger

Front Seat

Seat Guides

$\frac{3}{16}''$

Underside View

Wire Hanger

$\frac{1}{2}''$

$\frac{3}{8}''$

Step (pin)

$\frac{3}{8}''$

Brake Shoe

Nickel

$\frac{1}{8}''$

Covering

B

Beading

C

Beading

Back Curtain

Roof Covering

6. Glue the cross braces between the studs so the upper side is even with the upper ends of the studs.

7. Glue one of the lengthwise braces to the inside of the studs and the underside of the cross braces.

8. Fasten the roof supports to the upper side of the cross braces and the ends of the studs.

9. Glue the remaining roof support to the outside of the rear roof support, thus making that one double thickness.

10. Glue the back of the body to the two rear studs and upper edge of the box.

11. Make the side pieces for the rear seat by gluing the A piece to the B piece, allowing the B piece to extend ⅛″ at each end. Glue these assemblies (from the outside) to each side of the body between the last two studs and ⅝″ up from the upper edge of the box.

12. Glue the outside body braces to the last three studs 1⅜″ up from the edge of the box.

13. Glue one of the 1″ rear body studs to the outside of each rear corner stud between the roof support and upper edge of the back. Glue each of the other 1″ studs between the roof support and the edge of back ¼″ from the corner studs.

14. Make the seats by gluing the seat board to the seat back. Fasten a guide piece to the underside of the front seat ³⁄₁₆″ in from each end. The front seat slides on the seat supports.

15. Glue the rear seat to the back of the body and the seat supports.

16. Cover the roof supports with the slats spaced about ¹⁄₁₆″ apart.

17. Prepare the sides for the covering material by gluing

pieces of wood $\frac{1}{16}''$ x $\frac{1}{8}''$ by the length needed to the outside of the three rear side body studs. This will provide flat surfaces to fasten the covering to.

18. Drill a small hole in the center of the ends of each body hanger support to a depth of about $\frac{1}{4}''$. Glue these pieces to the underside of the box $\frac{1}{4}''$ in from each side. Shape the wire hangers from paper clips and insert the straight ends into the holes. The curved ends will fit over the bolsters.

19. Drill a small hole through the center of the end of each step support as shown. Glue the supports to each side of the underside of the box $\frac{5}{8}''$ from the front end.

20. Form the steps by pounding a piece of wire and bending it to shape or flatten the head of a large pin and bend it to the shape shown.

21. Shape the brake shoes with a half-round file. Glue a shoe to each end of the rod and fasten the rod to the body hanger holders $1\frac{1}{2}''$ from the back end with glue or pieces cut from small paper clips.

Covering the Buggy

A gray charcoal or pastel paper makes an excellent covering for the buggy. Other paper, including wallpaper, can be used and painted gray, but the charcoal paper gives the best results. Before covering the buggy, paint the box, back, front corner studs, and inside of the body black.

The following pieces will be needed for the covering:

2 pc $2\frac{3}{4}''$ x 3''—sides
1 pc $3\frac{1}{8}''$ x $4\frac{1}{4}''$—top
1 pc $\frac{1}{2}''$ x $2\frac{1}{2}''$—front roof support, piece A
1 pc $\frac{3}{8}''$ x $2\frac{1}{2}''$—back roof support, piece B

2 pc ½″ x 2¾″—back side pieces, C
1 pc 1⅝″ x 2¾″—back curtain
2 pc ⅛″ x 4″—sides ⎫
1 pc ⅛″ x 2½″—back ⎬ beading
⎭

1. Starting at the second stud from the front, glue each side piece to the studs, box, lower edge of roof, and filler pieces. The side pieces go down about ⅛″ onto the box. They will extend ¼″ beyond the rear stud. Crease and bend this end around the rear stud and glue it to the stud and back.

2. Glue the top piece to one side of the roof first. It will extend at the front and back about ⅛″. Apply glue to the roof and press the covering over it. Crease and bend the protruding ends down over the roof supports. Cut a small V-shaped piece from each corner so that it will fit better, and glue the covering to the supports.

3. Glue the two back strips C to the rear studs and back of the body. The lower ends of all pieces should be about ⅛″ down on the box, and all ends should be even.

4. Glue the curtain to the lower edge of the rear roof support. The curtain may be glued down or left glued only at the upper end so that it can be rolled up and held with two narrow paper straps. It can also be held in a closed position with short pieces cut from the head ends of small pins.

5. Glue the two roof support coverings, A and B, to the front and back supports. Trim around the curved ends of the roof with a scissors.

6. Glue the beading along the sides where the side and top piece meet. Glue the beading across the back at the same height as the side beading.

Materials for running gear:

   2 pc $\frac{3}{16}''$ x $\frac{3}{16}''$ x $3\frac{1}{2}''$—axletrees

   1 pc $\frac{1}{16}''$ x $\frac{3}{16}''$ x $1\frac{1}{2}''$—A

   2 pc $\frac{3}{16}''$ x $\frac{1}{2}''$ x $2\frac{3}{4}''$—for springs

   2 pc $\frac{3}{16}''$ x $\frac{3}{16}''$ x $2\frac{1}{2}''$—bolsters

   1 pc $\frac{3}{16}''$ x $\frac{3}{16}''$ x $1\frac{3}{4}''$—bed piece

   1 pc $\frac{1}{16}''$ x $\frac{3}{4}''$ x $\frac{1}{2}''$—for fifth wheel

   2 pc $\frac{1}{8}''$ x $\frac{3}{4}''$ x $6''$—for shafts

   1 pc $\frac{1}{8}''$ x $\frac{3}{16}''$ x $2\frac{1}{2}''$—x $\Big\}$ cross piece for shafts

   2 pc $\frac{1}{16}''$ x $\frac{3}{16}''$ x $2\frac{3}{4}''$—y

   1 pc $\frac{1}{8}''$ x $\frac{1}{8}''$ x $2''$—singletree

   2 pc $\frac{1}{16}''$ dowel $4\frac{5}{8}''$ long—tie rods

   2 paper clips

   2–$2\frac{3}{4}''$ wheels—rear

   2–$2\frac{1}{2}''$ wheels—front

   4 pins or small nails—axles

Construction:

1. Drill a hole for a pin in the center of each end of the axletrees to a depth of about $\frac{3}{8}''$.

2. Center piece A on the rear axletree and glue it fast. Drill no. 45 holes $1\frac{1}{4}''$ apart and $1\frac{1}{8}''$ from either end of the axletree for the tie rods.

3. Saw out the springs. See the diagram.

4. Round off the upper side of the bolsters.

5. Center and glue the spring to piece A on the rear axletree. Glue the rear bolster to the spring.

6. Drill holes at a and b in the front axletree for the shaft holders.

7. Glue the fifth wheel to the center of the front axletree.

8. Drill no. 45 holes in the bed piece $\frac{1}{4}''$ in from each end.

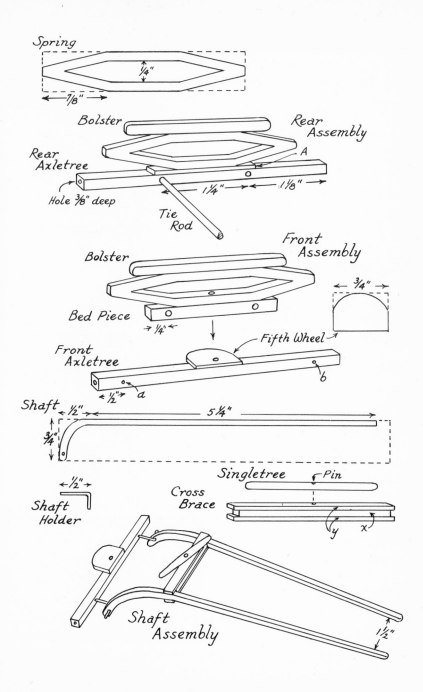

Spring

¼"

⅞"

Bolster

Rear
Assembly

Rear
Axletree

A

Hole ⅜" deep

1¼"

1⅛"

Tie
Rod

Bolster

Front
Assembly

Bed Piece

¾"

¼"

Front
Axletree

Fifth Wheel

½"   a

b

Shaft   ½"

5¼"

¾"

½"

Shaft
Holder

Cross
Brace

Singletree   Pin

y   x

Shaft
Assembly

1½"

9. Glue the bed piece to the lower side of the spring and the front bolster to the upper side.

10. Drill a hole for a pin through the center of the bed piece and lower side of the spring. Make a similar hole through the center of the front axletree and fifth wheel.

11. Insert a piece of wire or pin up through the axletree, fifth wheel, bed piece, and lower side of the spring. It should fit snugly in the holes.

12. Connect the rear axletree to the bed piece with the tie rods.

13. Saw out the shafts. Drill a no. 60 hole $\frac{1}{8}''$ from the curved end. Rub the ends of piece x on sandpaper to obtain a slight slant so that the shafts will point inward at the front ends, where they will be about $1\frac{1}{2}''$ apart. They should be about $2\frac{1}{2}''$ apart at the curved end. Make the cross brace by gluing piece x between the y pieces, which will extend $\frac{1}{8}''$ beyond x at each end. Drill a hole for a pin down through the center of the brace.

14. Set the brace between the shafts about $1\frac{1}{2}''$ from the curved end, and glue the shafts in the brace.

15. Make the singletree and fasten to the cross brace with a pin.

16. Attach the shafts to the hooks inserted into holes a and b in the front axletree. It is best to put the hooks into the shafts first and then into the axletree.

17. Paint the running gear black.

18. Mount the wheels. See the Introduction (pages 10–12).